Feminism in Africa

Critical South

The publication of this series is supported by the International Consortium of Critical Theory Programs funded by the Andrew W. Mellon Foundation.

Series editors: Natalia Brizuela, Victoria J. Collis-Buthelezi and Leticia Sabsay

Feminism in Africa

Gender, Knowledge and Resistance

Fatou Sow

With translations by Matthew B. Smith

polity

Polity Press
65 Bridge Street
Cambridge CB2 1UR, UK

Polity Press
111 River Street
Hoboken, NJ 07030, USA

ISBN-13: 978-1-5095-6773-7 – hardback
ISBN-13: 978-1-5095-6774-4 – paperback

A catalogue record for this book is available from the British Library.

Library of Congress Control Number: 2025948929

Typeset in 10.5 on 12pt Sabon
by Fakenham Prepress Solutions, Fakenham, Norfolk NR21 8NL
Printed and bound in Great Britain by Ashford Colour Ltd

The publisher has used its best endeavors to ensure that the URLs for external websites referred to in this book are correct and active at the time of going to press. However, the publisher has no responsibility for the websites and can make no guarantee that a site will remain live or that the content is or will remain appropriate.

Every effort has been made to trace all copyright holders, but if any have been overlooked the publisher will be pleased to include any necessary credits in any subsequent reprint or edition.

For further information on Polity, visit our website:
politybooks.com

Contents

CONCLUSION
AFRICAN FEMINISM NOW

Foreword

To the Lighthouse Keeper

Mame-Fatou Niang

Tata Fatou,

In Senegal, where you and I originated, the *Bàjjen* is the paternal aunt, a powerful figure vested with a host of social roles. She is the one who holds the newborn during the baptism and naming ceremonies, and she is central to the child's introduction to their community. Outside of their blood family, women can officiate as *Bàjjenu gox*, the godmothers of their neighborhood. Part confidant, part mentor, part auntie, the *Bàjjenu gox* is at once a person, a place and a feeling. She is a woman who brings comfort, the person who can hear one's secrets and untangle the roots of the deepest taboos, those that cannot be shared with a parent. The *Bàjjenu gox* is a place to learn, unwind, laugh or cry, be annoyed or joyous.

Tata Fatou, this is what you are to us, to generations of women in Africa and Black girls in the diaspora who learned with you that it was okay to be different and have questions, okay to say no and raise one's voice. You are *Bàjjen* to generations of women in Africa and Black girls in the diaspora who learned with you that these questions were not figments of our imagination: the tremors we felt in our bodies, the silences nested in our native tongues, and the shadows of elaborated traditions. In you, we found the comfort of a lighthouse and sketches of livable futures. After years of waiting, I am grateful to Polity Press for publishing this first compilation in English of your remarkable body of work. This book, *Feminism in Africa*, presents articles and interviews published between 1997 and 2019. It illuminates the lives of women navigating from the intimacy of the gynaeceum to rural fields to African metropolises; from anti-colonial fervor to post-independence blues to neocolonial realities.

Tata, you write from the unique vantage point of a *témoin de son temps*, a witness of her time and a pioneer of gender studies on the continent. In 1960, with your father's encouragement, you became one of the first female students at Dakar's Cheikh Anta Diop University (one of only two women in that freshman class). In 1988, you would deliver there the first course on African feminism ever offered at the institution. While traveling across the world to lecture on women in African contexts, you helped set up the first research groups dedicated to studying the structures that shape the lives of African women. The Réseau de recherche sur la santé de la reproduction en Afrique francophone (Network of Research on Reproductive Health in Francophone Africa, 1989), the Gender Institute at CODESRIA (1994), the Francophone Africa chapter of the Development Alternatives with Women for a New Era (DAWN) and the African Feminist Forum are among a handful of networks that you founded or joined to expose the role of gender in the marginalization of women. More than 60 years after entering the university in Dakar, and despite your retirement from academia, you still travel the globe tirelessly to celebrate victories, raise alarms and propose solutions for fairer futures. Tata, you are a monument for generations of researchers and activists, the blueprint of our feminist engagement. We are forever grateful for your commitment and for these records that you kept rigorously. This present collection is an invaluable legacy.

I discovered your work in the mid-2000s while completing a Master's in the United States. Before that, I had attended college in France to study architecture and literature with a comprehensive minor in gender studies. In three years, our program never stepped out of Europe and North America. Those courses left me with the impression that, from Olympe de Gouges to Seneca Falls to our times, feminism had been a science from, by and for white women.

Tata, the internet says that you lived 502 kilometers away from me, the distance between Paris where you taught and Lyon where I lived. Yet I had to cross the Atlantic and travel 5,586 kilometers to the United States to encounter you. To this day, I still feel the many sensations that came with seeing your name on an American syllabus, the feelings that came with learning about your work: clarity, a sense of belonging and resolve. That course syllabus is framed in my office in lieu of my doctoral diploma. It is my way of honoring a document that introduced me to you, to Tata Awa Thiam, to Maryse Condé, Aimé Césaire, Fanon and to so many others. When I assign your work, I encourage students to think about these silences in Western canonical humanities. How do certain absences affect our understanding of ourselves and of the world? How do we heal from these amputations? How do we place ourselves on the path to being whole again, on the road to reconnecting with the many circles rendered invisible by Western modernity?

Soo ko seetluwul, yoonam du yomb.
If you neglect the little girl, her path will not be easy.

Tata Fatou, you cared for us. Reading you alongside Guadeloupe's Maryse Condé and Senegal's Awa Thiam was my introduction to transnational feminism, an ethic of sisterhood grounded in an anti-capitalist and anti-patriarchal ethos. You led me to Caribbean, African, Black feminist and Afro-feminist thinkers such as Gail Lewis, Jacqui Alexander, Makeda Silvera, Jeanne Martin Cissé, Ifi Amadiume, Amina Mama and Oyèrónkẹ Oyéwùmí. Reading you allowed me to discover and place myself within a genealogy of Black women who dared to think freely about their bodies, creativity, sex, pleasure and their right to simply exist.

Feminism in Africa is an original introduction to the practice of feminism in African contexts. This collection of articles outlines the social means through which African women have been disempowered and maintained at the margins. It chronicles their political mobilization with a wealth of names, dates and places. This book is also a toolbox theorizing the universal from the perspective of women in Africa. In it, you rigorously present the development of gender studies on the continent, debunking the myths of a Western import and the impossible Africanness of feminism. When you frame your reflections around human rights, you brilliantly demonstrate how African women's rights to enjoy their bodies, to not suffer in their bodies or because of their bodies, ultimately raise questions of dignity and equal rights for all. Collaborating with feminists across the world, you propose methods to co-construct knowledge between shareholders with different interests. As an academic invested in epistemic justice, you dissect the reception in the West of knowledge produced in Africa and by Africans. On African campuses, you highlight the continued resistance to the inclusion of gender in social studies and, generally, of knowledge produced outside academic circles. Beyond its value as an archive written by a central protagonist of this history, this book encourages its readers to consider humanity in light of knowledge produced from Africa, by African women.

Tata, you teach us that feminism cannot be singular as it naturally adapts to the demands and material conditions of its location. If all feminisms have in common to defend the rights of women mistreated because of their gender, you call for the recognition of African specificities. To successfully unmask the structures that have naturalized the inferiority of women, one needs to consider several elements, such as the sheer number of countries in the second largest continent in the world; the potency of myths and traditions in contemporary African societies; ethnicity and caste systems, class, lineage, parenting and the interpretations of the maternal, etc. African intersectionality requires an analysis of these elements in their systemic relation to precolonialism, colonialism and neoliberalism.

At once a historian and a pillar of gender studies' early institutionalization in Africa, you give us an account of their birth against a backdrop of erasure and conservatism. Yet this book does not just chronicle setbacks, pain and struggles. It is a receptacle of beauty, a cartography of African joy nested in everyday life and ordinary gestures. You generously acquaint us with the efforts of your feminist sisters: Amina Mama, Filomena Chioma Steady, Buchi Emecheta, Nawal el-Saadawi, Mercy Amba-Odudoye, Oyèrónkẹ Oyéwùmí, Achola Pala, Madina Ly, Patricia McFadden and Fatima Mernissi. You also introduce us to innumerable networks of ordinary and anonymous faces who made the movement: women in NGOs, tontines, microcredit hubs, markets, political parties and associations; women who fought against genital mutilation, polygamy, forced marriage and gender-based violence. Your book is a trove of acronyms, a call to remember names that have fallen into oblivion, and to celebrate everyday women who understood feminism as radical, collective and anchored in a situated practice. Tata, I learned from you that many of these women did not call themselves feminist, but they feminism-ed. Your analyses of gender and African intersectionalities illuminate feminism not just as a posture that is claimed, but rather as a way of being. The African women in your work were not simply feminist, they actively practiced feminism.

From community circles to international organizations, you show African women's sustained mobilization to assert their citizenship as well as the rights attached to it. Your work is an extraordinary tale of decades of efforts against the political misogyny that stalled women's public presence. Tata, you show that this was nothing natural, nothing that owed to an innate inferiority of women. In post-independence Africa, a well-oiled system fueled by a social fear of women's power worked full throttle to establish "Republics without female citizens." By showing the significant gaps between women's presence in independentist movements and their meager roles in the new states' governing bodies, your book exposes the inner workings of this erasure.

You analyze the reduction of African women's bodies to their reproductive functions, and their transformation into sites regulated by the community. Although difficult, mobilizations for women's rights were spontaneous in the fight against early pregnancy, force-feeding or polygamy, while genital mutilations remained largely untouched until the mid-1990s. For you, the weight of social taboos, shame and a fear of amalgamation explain this late awakening. Indeed, African women, researchers and women's advocacy organizations were late to speak out against female genital mutilation (FGM) out of modesty, but also for fear of validating stereotypes on the "backwardness" of African societies. Your handling of the issue has been a lesson in pedagogy and radical love. By moving the cursor from the cultural to the legal, you centered women's right to dispose of their bodies. Your article "Female Genital Mutilation and Human Rights" (1998) is a staple of my teaching. Whether in a course on Black Feminisms or a seminar on Universalism, your work remains an example of sensible and incorruptible thought. Indeed, in order to defuse the cultural issue, you place the FGM debate on the terrain of women's rights, thus transforming the legal system into a tool at women's disposal. Your intervention on language is as timely. When you encourage your reader to shift the cultural issue contained in popular expressions such as "female circumcision" and to use the word "mutilation," you highlight the loss of integrity brought on by the operation. The very act of naming displaces the conversation from traditional practices to a serious attack on the dignity of the body. These lessons are valuable in guiding us when we are torn between the opposite sides of a cause, when we are tempted to turn a blind eye to an injustice rather than condemning the marginalized group that commits it. You teach us to focus radically on dignity and the right of people to have ownership of their bodies.

In the 1970s, the appropriation of gender studies and their inclusion in social sciences took place in patriarchal, masculine and religious African societies still marked by colonial legacies. Your actions were seen as activist passions contrary to academic reason, and frivolous demands compared to the pressing issues faced by the new sovereign countries. When your detractors prioritized the transmission of national identity, pedagogy of citizenship, the construction of national pride and economic self-sufficiency, you admirably demonstrated that women's rights were not just included in these existential questions. Far from being an end goal, equality between men and women was a condition *sine qua non* for achieving the "Suns of Independence."

Tata, I learned from you that it was okay to talk about oneself, to talk from oneself and one's place in the world. As academia lionized axiological neutrality and pushed back against the use of the pronoun "I," you fiercely spoke in the first-person, grounding your research in the most intimate corners of your lived experience. Your autoethnography of a feminist scholar in African and Western academia gives vivid details about your difficulties. Yet this resistance seems to have strengthened your resolve to speak up and to challenge gendered subjugation in all its forms. You insist on the need to advocate for oneself when women's intersectional needs are ignored. The work contained in this book is a precious toolbox for us as we are creating spaces to share the sources, inspirations, methods for our studies; places where we can test out our disciplines' ability to respond to pressing issues faced by women on the continent, and ultimately by humanity. Your words invite us to become and remain undisciplined.

Your six decades of research are extraordinarily attuned to our times 25 years into the century. Religious conservatism is surging and tightening throughout the continent. Nationalist myths and traditions are exposed in debates that illuminate the tensions between universalist principles and the reality of their application. Unable or unwilling to face these contradictions, our societies increasingly hide behind patriarchal postures and ethnonationalist jargons where words are thrown around, emptied out, narrowed down to the point of losing their meaning. Your work is a critical intervention that reinvests in language, radical (self-)love, faith and the power of collective action.

Tata, the fight continues.

More than 60 years after gender perspectives' introduction on African campuses, the opposition is still strong. We still have to explain that biological differences do not naturally carry hierarchies between the sexes and that there are indeed African specificities in the way these hierarchies are organized. You invite us to focus less on proving the others wrong, and more on looking at the big picture. Our actions are to improve the lives of women, but, ultimately, highlighting gender in the construction of social inequalities provides tools to understand other social mechanisms of domination and marginalization. In that sense, your work is a universal tool for social justice that aims to identify, deconstruct and eliminate all forms of domination, using gender-based domination as a model.

Tata, at times, it is painful to read what you had to go through: the gaslighting and the hurt that you lay out with grace in hope that we will learn how to avoid them. Thanks to you, we can memorize the maps that you designed with careful precision, learn the routes of solidarity and avoid the traps. You also invite us to wonder what it means to build or create "new" fields of study in this Millennium: How "new" are these fields? How do we avoid the pitfalls of "Columbusing," "firsting" and constantly reinventing the wheel? How do we identify and take care of our archives in order to account for the works already created by people like you? How do we account for the knowledge produced by ordinary women operating outside our institutions' realms? In a world with increasing borders, how do we ensure a fair circulation of people and resources? How do we develop translation to democratize epistemic influence across the planet?

One question links these interrogations: "Who are we doing this for – who do we want to do this for?" In your vision, the relationship with African women will remain an essential foundation of African women's studies, a field born from struggles waged well beyond our campuses. You center the accessibility of academic writings and findings. This accessibility should not only be tied to the reduction or elimination of scientific jargon and the circulation of scholarly productions outside academic circles, but must extend to companionship with people outside the university. As you state so powerfully, the individual stories of success and the proliferation of academic courses or conferences should neither be an end goal, nor hide the immensity of what is left to achieve. The fight for gender equality is a radical gesture toward justice and dignity for all.

The lights are on. The lighthouse and her companions have enlightened the path. Sisters, we can move forward.

Tata, when I read your testimony on these decades of mobilization, I realize the progress made in a host of areas, from health to legal rights to the very presence of gender in public debates. I realize how vital the constant pressure had been to break the taboos around child marriage, polygamy or genital mutilations. I also measure the failures – what has been gained then subsequently lost, what is still to be improved. Yet reading you brings hope for the future. Reading you cements the conviction that our current circumstances are not a starting point, that we are not starting from scratch. You show us that the mobilizations of those who came before us have borne fruits. You armed my generation with archives, paths and faith. You mapped out a number of dangers lurking away and warned us to remain alert. Do not worry, Tata. We are listening and we are taking notes. We know about the water leaks, the cracks in the boat and the giant waves ahead. We remain calm and reassured by your presence. You are our beacon in the night.

Tata, I have raised many questions in this letter, but remember, you said that it was okay to have questions. I now invite the reader to settle into the next pages and discover your generous words. I am grateful for this reader. I hope that this mosaic of articles, interviews and lectures takes a wide readership through your radical, transnational and African feminist paths toward freedom. It is a generous work of citations, an archive of African feminist movements anchored in the voices of women from Dakar to Ndjamena, a gift magnified by its potential as a toolbox for global liberation. *Feminism in Africa* is a site of love and pain, laughter and tears, transmission and futures. These futures are not merely to be imagined, as they are grounded in the past/paths that you reveal. We are here, because you have been there *Bàjjen*.

Delloo naa la njukkal, Tata.

Thank you for everything. Thank you for showing us the way so we know "who to recognize when the earth shakes on the last day."

Introduction

Becoming a feminist was a life's journey. Raising feminist questions while the socio-cultural, economic and political future of Africa was being debated was an immense challenge. It remains so, as our contemporary African societies and their relationship with the world in these uncertain times have only grown more complex.

In the early 1980s, when the ongoing struggles of African women were beginning to be viewed through a feminist lens, we were met head on with countless obstacles. Was it even possible to self-identify as a feminist, to lay claim to the term? It was a difficult, uncomfortable and even politically hazardous stance to take given the resistance and suspicion it provoked, charged as it was with being imported from elsewhere, a prefab ideology ill suited to local realities. The African intelligentsia, in particular, questioned its political and ideological underpinnings. Did it make sense for me, an African intellectual and a woman from a particular social class, to speak on behalf of other women, on behalf of the great masses of women from working-class or rural backgrounds? This symbolic and political confinement to an ivory tower, shielded from local miseries, rendered us incapable of understanding the everyday realities on the ground, thanks to this arbitrarily constructed hierarchy of knowledge, as some critics pointed out. At that time, it was considered inappropriate to judge, from a feminist viewpoint labeled as Westernized – as using Western eyes – and hegemonic, the highly politicized, even nationalist, production of African knowledge.

African women had to develop a uniquely African perspective on women and their societies while refusing the feminist label. This was in response to the developmentalist discourse on women, which has been widely criticized for its arrogance and universalist stance. We were to decolonize knowledge, to lay out more consequential objectives. Just as the African production of knowledge aimed, for example, to "set African history on its feet," a motto among African women was to "prioritize our priorities." But this was no easy task. How were we to respond to the vindictive mockery from male-dominated strongholds in academia, the dismissals from both male and female public opinion, the near-*fatwas* from religious figures? How to deal with the repudiations from women's organizations or the pushback from high-powered women who held senior government or university positions?

This collection of articles illustrates my own journey through this global discourse. I haven't dedicated space to every ideological battle, to every theoretical and political stance on feminism and issues of women, sex and gender, nor the pushback or silence encountered along the way. Instead, I have highlighted several points that demonstrate the emergence and development of women's and feminist studies in African research, with its achievements, failures and, most importantly, its complexity.

Amina Mama (1996) at the Council for the Development of Social Science Research in Africa (CODESRIA), and Désirée Lewis (2002) at the African Gender Institute, have documented and commented on the growing production and quality of scholarship, both within universities and among networks and organizations of women. This work has enabled the "institutionalization of their presence and thus the articulation of the agenda of African feminism, facilitating research and activism by African women scholars" (Mama 1996:6).

Several recent studies have shown the evolution of African women's and feminist studies, both within the continent and internationally. My thinking has been deeply influenced by all the discussions that have emphasized the transnational dimensions of various global issues. This includes the challenges of education and employment, the impact of globalization on economies and workforce development, government relations and civic engagement, health and sexual and reproductive rights, the influence of religions, and the rise of fundamentalism.

I often wonder if we are constructing our analytical frameworks, searching for colonial and global sources of sexism and discrimination against women, without giving enough consideration to their African contexts and variations. It is crucial to examine the influence of patriarchy in light of Africa's historical matriarchal systems, which form the basis of the continent's social structures. We should also evaluate how gender intersects with age, class, ethnicity, caste, race and religious disparities, among other inequalities prevalent on the continent. We must delve into these matters as well as others that affect us on a more personal level.

Nearly 20 years ago, the African Feminist Forum adopted feminism "without any ifs, ands, or buts," based on clear principles: "By calling ourselves feminists, we are politicizing the struggle for women's rights, we are challenging the legitimacy of the structures that keep women subjugated, and we are developing tools for analysis and transformative actions" (2006:4).

In these pages, I have tried to retrace the difficult path we took as we adopted a feminist vision that resonates deeply with us as African women and connects with other women globally who share our aspirations and struggles. Too often, we have retreated to "gender" as a safe space; some have distorted or exploited this concept, reducing it to a simplistic, misunderstood term (does it refer to women, or both men and women?). It has become diluted, non-confrontational and pleasingly accommodating – in fact, overly accommodating. Gender, once a forceful feminist concept describing the power dynamics between men and women (a source of domination and inequality), has become a weak descriptor, sometimes referring only to women, other times to relations between men and women without any critical perspective. It is essential to restore the power and precision of this concept from a feminist standpoint.

I am an African feminist, rooted in my African context, in my African cultures which I claim the right to interpret and reinterpret. I feel compelled to collect stories – ancient, contemporary and still to come – to document our evolving values (for they are alive). I see it as my duty to analyze conflicting realities, transformations, and contradictions, as well as the complex contributions that are specific to different times and

places. Our cultures are not just relics of our struggles against a
colonial West, a West defined by domination. Our cultures are
primarily our memories and our living spaces that we reinvent
daily, at every moment, with each generation. Our cultures are
actively constructed, deconstructed and reconstructed, marked
by triumphs and defeats.

At its core, feminism examines the conditions of women and
the mechanisms that enable and enforce the various forms of
their oppression. It also acts to abolish these forms of oppression
through political action. Being a feminist means striving to
change the power dynamics between the sexes, to promote their
equality in law, and to enhance access to citizenship for all,
including women. All feminist theories have placed the same
emphasis on the oppression of women, although they vary in
their analysis of its causes, manifestations, language and impacts.
Feminism consistently condemns sexism, a form of discrimination based on sex that contributes to women's oppression,
marginalization, invisibility and exclusion.

I know that our work is far from finished. It has only just
begun. Our efforts are being taken up by the younger generation
and will continue to be led by generations that follow. They will
likely continue to confront discrimination against women that
stubbornly persists alongside otherwise evolving circumstances.

PART ONE
AFRICAN FEMINISMS
CHARTING FEMINIST MOVEMENTS, DOING FEMINIST RESEARCH

1

The Political Mobilization of Women in West Africa: Forms, Sites and Contemporary Stakes (2005)[1]

From groups born out of community life and based on sex, age and/or ethnic or religious affiliation, to professional associations of the first graduates from colonial schools, and contemporary human rights advocacy groups, a whole spectrum of women's organizations have left their mark on African political life. Initially, at the start of the various independence movements, these often aligned with political parties, unions and other mass movements, sometimes even emerging from them. With the rise of civil society organizations in the 1980s, these groups multiplied in a more self-directed manner. In any case, they have had a dramatic impact on the history of women since the calls for independence.

It is now recognized that 30 years of debates and diverse supportive actions directed at women have significantly contributed to their mobilization and their involvement at various levels. To be sure, by the early 1970s, the key issues affecting women globally, their impact on women's conditions, and the strategies crafted to address them, were defined primarily by the Global North.[2] But due to differences in context and perspective, the women's movement has fragmented into a multitude of groups that express its diversity and richness. Today, African women, like other women from the Global South, have grounded their mobilization in their local realities, focusing primarily on issues pertinent to their communities. They have fortified their positions through encounters and confrontations with other groups. And while, during the era of decolonization, they found meager support from single-party governments, they now have a voice in politics and can make their demands clear, although they still face challenges in executing their electoral promises and making politicians follow through on their commitments.

This chapter explores the factors driving women's political mobilization in recent history by addressing several key questions: Where, why and how have women mobilized politically? In short, what do we mean when we speak of their political mobilization? What have been the forms and sites of this mobilization? What have been the major goals and challenges faced amidst various political, economic and cultural shifts and restructurings, particularly over the past two decades? Have two decades dedicated to women by the United Nations provided more clarity on the various constraints they face, or in any way mitigated the impact of these constraints? Have these years fostered strategies for improving their situation and achieving greater equality? Assessing the political engagement of women during these decades, especially since the Beijing Conference in 1995, remains a challenge. This is due to the very diversity of women's political engagement and the impact of a global environment marked by vast political and social transformations. This analysis aims to identify the gains and setbacks since the 1995 World Conference on Women in Beijing. As many had feared, the tenuousness of these achievements remained a significant concern at the Cairo and Beijing +10 conferences.

1.1 Women's Participation in Politics Before the Promises of the United Nations Decade for Women

Ghana and Guinea-Conakry were undoubtedly the pioneers in championing women's rights in West Africa, starting from their independence as a result of forceful anti-colonial campaigns. After achieving international sovereignty in March 1957, Ghana saw a politically tumultuous period marked by several military coups. Between 1960 and 1965, Kwame Nkrumah, the country's first president, actively promoted women's participation in government. He included several women in the Central Committee of the Convention People's Party (CPP) and designated 3 out of 103 parliamentary seats for women. He also appointed them as city council members and district commissioners.[3] He appointed them as leaders of administrative services, schools and significant institutions, and placed them on the boards of major national companies (Tsikata 1997:392). However, these efforts were not sustained. By the 2nd Republic (1972–4), just prior to the United Nations Decade for Women, only 2 women were members of the 140-seat Ghanaian Parliament.

At that time, Guinea was the first country to achieve this level of breakthrough for women, largely thanks to the support of charismatic leaders whom women had helped bring to power. Refusing to participate in the Franco-African community proposed by General de Gaulle, the country gained independence in October 1958. True to his commitment to women during his tenure as a trade unionist and later as a political leader of the Rassemblement Démocratique Africain (RDA), Sékou Touré placed them in senior political and professional roles (Guillaume 2000). This was clearly a legacy of the women's activism within the RDA. The president argued that:

> The Guinean revolution cannot achieve its full effect, nor fully develop, if a portion of the population remains on the margins of the national renovation effort we have undertaken. The more men, women and youth we engage, the more wills and initiatives we gather, and the faster we will accelerate not only our own evolution but also the evolution of Africa. (Qtd. in Guillaume 2000:79)

Between 1958 and 1984, Guinea promoted several women to high-ranking roles, including as ministers, deputies and ambassadors. Jeanne Martin Cissé, a notable minister and parliamentarian, was the first woman to preside over the United Nations General Assembly.[4] Women also held executive positions in senior administration and local government, led national companies and served as mayors and district chiefs. Additionally, they occupied roles in specialized police and military units, which are usually closed to women in many other countries.

Despite the significant role of women in Nigeria's pre-colonial political history and their involvement in liberation struggles, the Nigerian federal government granted them only a minimal place, although recognizing their rights to vote and stand for elections (suffrage). In 1960, only one female representative for Southern Nigeria was recruited into Parliament. The following year saw a slight increase, with one woman appointed to the local assembly in Southern Nigeria and three in Eastern Nigeria. It wasn't until 1979 that a woman was elected to the assembly of the Muslim-dominated Northern Nigeria, following the country's return to civilian rule. From that date forward, their numbers began to grow, although they remained very small in these local bodies. Also in 1979, under the federal government of the Second Republic, the first two women were appointed to the federal government, one as the minister of national planning and internal affairs, and the other as permanent secretary (Attoe 1996:4).

In other countries of the sub-region, women's ascension to parliamentary and ministerial positions occurred later, despite their active membership in political parties. The first Republic of Mali, under Modibo Keïta (1960–8), did not appoint any women to the National Assembly or assign them any government roles, despite their involvement in the RDA. It was not until the second Republic (1968–91), which arose from a military coup, that efforts were made to "promote" the political and professional status of women. Shortly after assuming power in 1968, after the military coup – and eight years before the United Nations Decade for Women – President Moussa Traoré appointed a woman as secretary of state for social affairs. During his tenure, four women were given ministerial positions. The political office of the only party, the Union Démocratique du Peuple Malien (UDPM), included three women under the national women's movement, and the legislative bodies saw an increase in female representation with five women in Parliament, one in the National Council, and six in the Economic and Social Council (Ba Konaré 1993:66). Despite these advances, a gender bias remained in administrative roles; Article 16 of the statute regarding general administrative personnel explicitly stated that, while the administrative corps was open to both sexes, regional command functions were reserved for male administrators (Ba Konaré 1993:62).

In Senegal, three years after gaining independence in 1960, the first female parliamentarian, Caroline Diop, a teacher and alumna of the renowned girls' school L'École normale de

Rufisque, was elected (or rather co-opted) in 1963. It wasn't until the 1973–8 legislature – a full ten years later – that four additional women joined the Parliament (Sow and Guèye 2000:156). The first cabinet positions for women were introduced in 1978 as part of an effort to promote and empower women. In Togo, women entered the National Assembly for the first time in 1961. Unsurprisingly, these women had been strong supporters of the country's first president, Sylvanus Olympio. In Côte d'Ivoire, despite their strong support for Houphouët-Boigny's policies, only three women joined the assembly in 1963. The first female minister and mayor were appointed in 1976, just after the 1975 International Women's Year. This pattern of gradual female political inclusion was echoed across the sub-region. In Mauritania, a woman became a parliamentarian for the first time in 1975, during the International Year. Burkina Faso – formerly Upper Volta – saw its first female parliamentarians in 1978, followed by Benin in 1979, Gambia in 1982, and Niger in 1988. In Guinea-Bissau and Cape Verde, former Portuguese colonies that achieved independence later than neighboring countries, a few women entered Parliament between 1972 and 1975. From the initial two to three female members in early legislatures, the number increased to eight to ten by the period between 1994 and 2003.

Political parties, both ruling and in opposition, included few women in their leadership from 1960 to 1975.[5] Research into women's political engagement reveals their high mobilization within single-party regimes and male-dominated elites; however, they rarely attain senior leadership roles. The colonial system had already marginalized them by establishing restrictive criteria for political participation, such as citizenship and the right to vote. And even after gaining independence, women did not rise to leadership positions in the new political structures. They were often confined to roles that aligned with a "male vision of politics" [*imaginaire politique masculin*], situated within a republican framework that largely excluded female citizens (Diaw 1998:12).

Women's access to political leadership in Senegal, as in other parts of the sub-region and likely around the world, faces significant challenges. An analysis in the report "Les Sénégalaises en chiffres" ["Senegalese Women by Numbers"] highlights the issue clearly:

Despite their demographic significance and active mobilization, women remain largely absent from leadership roles due to prevailing societal inertia. This inertia is reflected in conservative attitudes and behaviors within Senegalese society that resist acknowledging gender equality at leadership levels. The community struggles with the notion of women gaining power, fearing it might lead to female dominance. Many women have internalized their "subordination" under a patriarchal system, further reinforced by civil and religious laws, which has created a significant barrier to achieving legal gender equality. (Sow and Guèye 2000:155)

Women's opportunities to participate in decision-making were restricted because both ruling and opposition parties co-opted them. Despite some resistance, a tacit alliance that formed among all parties, rooted in political misogyny, forced women's organizations to conform to, or merge with, prevailing power structures, which had previously co-opted earlier women's movements. The first female parliamentarians were appointed as part of a so-called national movement that, despite its name, was controlled by a single party.

As Adam Ba Konaré points out, in Mali,

the various women's associations established during the colonial period were dissolved because, at that time, no issue in Africa could be discussed outside the political context. [...] The regime of the Union Soudanaise – Rassemblement Démocratique Africain (US–RDA), also known as the Sudanese Union – African Democratic Rally (1960–1968), opposed the formation of a true national women's union in Mali. Instead, in 1962, it only set up a commission, named the Social Commission of Women of Mali, which included eighteen members and was represented in the party by its General Secretary, Aoua Keïta, and chaired by Mariam Travélé. (1993:55)

Mariam Travélé was the wife of the incumbent president. During this decade, the influence of First Ladies became particularly pronounced, serving as a means to control populations through the resources and programs they managed, thereby securing their loyalty. For other female leaders, while some earned their positions through their organizing activities, others were appointed or co-opted by the ruling power, a clear indication of cronyism.

Based on the analysis of women's organizations and their political representation up to 1975, it is clear that the initiatives from that period until the 1995 Beijing Conference acted as catalysts for their mobilization and ascent to power. Despite their political mobilization being somewhat disorganized due to numerous restructurings, both continentally and globally, it laid the foundation for all other forms of mobilization (Taylor 2000).[6] Keeping these factors in mind helps us to better understand the successes and shortcomings of this mobilization and to better address the impact of Beijing +10.

1.2 Women's Organizations in the United Nations Decade for Women: A Giant Step Forward in Politics

The significance of the scale and diversity of an African women's movement, unified by common concerns, cannot be overstated. This movement reached its peak during the United Nations Decade for Women (1975–85), followed by two decades (1985–95 and 1995–2005) marked by phases of consolidation and evaluation of achievements. The global community was unmistakably energized by feminist and women's advocacy groups championing their causes. International cooperation played a crucial role in organizing and funding this mobilization. In preparation for each global conference of the Decade, the United Nations system, supported by bilateral partnerships, facilitated numerous national and local conferences. These served as regional preparatory meetings where future participants could discuss key issues and strategize on improving women's conditions and rights. Away from official government meeting venues, women's associations and non-governmental organizations gradually made their presence and voices felt. Despite their influential discourse on women's freedoms and rights, their innovative concepts (such as gender) and powerful slogans ("Women's rights are human rights"), their efforts were often co-opted by the authorities, typically without any genuine effort to implement their priorities.

It is important to recognize that the mobilization of women was part of a broader organizational movement, which was predominantly led by men. During the promising democratic transitions that marked the end of dictatorships, starting in the late 1980s, the "disqualification" of African states by Western governments and international institutions paved the way for the rise of civil society. This new civil society consisted of a complex array of multifaceted movements. Women's organizations, in particular, gained strength from their affiliation with a global women's movement, a connection that was not as pronounced before and immediately after independence.

> The women's movement does indeed resemble a constantly growing and shifting cobweb, one made up of thousands of large and small, local, national, regional, and international women's groups and organisations, connected and unconnected to each other and involved in traditional and non-traditional activities. What all these women's groups and organisations have in common is that for the most part they have been left out of the history of development as currently written. (Walker 2000:133)

The growing activism among women has led to the creation of new structures specifically designed to meet their material, social and political needs. These structures have established solution-oriented frameworks that concentrate on critical areas such as education access for women, economic integration, political participation and the fight against violence – including domestic violence, sexual abuse and female genital mutilation. Over time, these initiatives have progressively framed their demands within the broader context of a human right to development. Today, women worldwide are not only addressing these issues more effectively but also becoming more skilled at articulating their challenges, developing strategies, and, in some cases, securing funding.

Traditional organizations have been complemented by a wide range of new groups, from friendship circles to NGOs, which provide platforms for women's voices and offer spaces where they can pursue their ambitions. These organizations are dedicated to training and educating women, raising awareness about women's rights, and facilitating access to microfinance tools to foster the development of rural and urban activities. Notable examples include the Association pour la promotion de la femme sénégalaise (APROFES) in Senegal, the Association des femmes pour le développement (AfeDeM) and the Association malienne pour la sauvegarde du bien-être familial (AMASBIF) in Mali. Other organizations have emerged more specifically as spaces of resistance against physical and sexual violence against women, including domestic violence, genital mutilation and other forms of abuse. These include the Comité de lutte contre la violence envers les femmes (CLVF) in Senegal, the Association malienne pour la santé et l'optimisation des populations traditionnelles (AMSOPT) in Mali, the Comité Burkina pour la défense des femmes (CBDF) in Burkina Faso, and the Action pour l'Indépendance des dames (AID) in Côte d'Ivoire. These groups have mobilized to ban practices that are harmful to the health of mothers and children, especially female genital mutilation (FGM). Organizations have also addressed health, sexuality and fertility issues, focused on family well-being, often in partnership with the International Planned Parenthood Federation (IPPF) based in the UK. Examples include the Association sénégalaise pour le bien-être familial (ASBEF) in Senegal and the Association guinéenne pour le bien-être familial (AGBF) in Guinea-Conakry. The plight of widows and orphans, who face emotional, legal and economic challenges rooted in cultural practices, has not been overlooked. Organizations like the Association des veuves et orphelins du Burkina Faso (AVOB) and similar institutions across West and Central Africa offer legal support to these vulnerable groups, helping them combat expropriations and other injustices related to inheritance, while also providing training to bolster their financial and material independence.

How have women's organizations framed their demands and achieved success? To what extent have political parties been effective in amplifying women's voices? By organizing themselves, women's movements within both ruling and opposition parties have been able to position their struggles and demands within the democratic space as full citizens. In the absence of parity or significant representation in the political sphere, how have they managed to make their voices heard and to position gender as a significant concern within the dominant discourse?

1.3 The Political Mobilization of Women: The Legacy of the United Nations Decade for Women

The political mobilization of women gained such momentum from the United Nations Decade for Women that it now seems crucial to assess its impact following the landmark 1995 Beijing Conference. Demands for gender equality, expressed at local, national and international levels, have compelled political leaders to increase women's visibility significantly. The organizations discussed earlier have not only fueled public discourse on gender issues but have also strived to shatter the "glass ceiling" – or break free from the "iron chains" – that have hindered their progress. Undoubtedly, this surge in women's active participation has been bolstered by the momentum generated during the Decade. Since 1975, women have progressively attained key roles in government, securing positions as ministers and parliamentarians, as well as leadership roles in both the public and private sectors. However, countries that initially championed women's rights after independence have often struggled to maintain this early momentum, perhaps reflecting the strategies used by ruling elites to constrain the movement.

In Ghana, during the Third Republic (1979–81), the number of women in Parliament increased to only five, despite earlier promises made during the United Nations Decade for Women. As in Mali, there was a crackdown on organizations that had supported the previous regime. Prominent female business leaders, who had been supporters of Nkrumah, faced accusations of various wrongdoings, such as price manipulation and corruption of officials. They were subject to periodic persecution, which ranged from administrative and economic harassment to physical violence (Tsikata 1997:411). Under the military regime led by Jerry Rawlings, harsh actions were justified under the pretext that a powerful class of businessmen and businesswomen were causing price hikes and product shortages. At the same time, Rawlings' wife, Nana Konadu Agyeman, founded the 31st December Women's Movement (31st DWM) as an arm of her husband's "revolution." Like the spouses of leaders from other countries, she positioned her movement at the forefront of the limited space allocated for women's organizations. Particularly after the political party ban was lifted in 1992, she used this space to advance her political positions. Her movement not only occupied this space but also actively opposed other women's organizations that were advocating against discrimination and violence toward women by the regime, eventually eclipsing these groups (Tsikata 1997).

A decade after major global conferences, there were some political breakthroughs for Ghanaian women. In the 1992 parliamentary elections, out of 23 candidates, 16 women were elected to a 200-member Parliament after 11 years of military rule. This figure remained the same in the 1996 elections. However, as highlighted by Charlotte Binka, a Ghanaian reporter, there was a decline in women's representation, as 57 candidates ran in these elections, and women made up 49.5 percent of the electorate (1996:2). In the 2000 parliamentary elections, there were 2 more women elected, totaling 18 seats held by women. According to Binka, the first Ghanaian woman to run in the 1996 presidential elections managed to defeat two out of six candidates, despite being dismissed as having no chance and being widely considered "crazy," including by women (1996:2).

In Guinea, 20 years after the death of Sékou Touré (1984) and the military coup of Lansana Conté,[7] who remained in power for a long time, Guinean women witnessed the gains of the "revolution" erode. These gains were not effectively replaced by advancements expected from the United Nations Decade for Women, despite women's active involvement in its campaigns. In the 1995 legislative elections, there were only 10 women among 114 deputies, less than 9 percent of the seats. This number increased to 22 in the 2002 elections. The number of female cabinet members dropped to 4 during the 2000 administrative restructuring.[8] These reports also highlight a regression of women in decision-making positions in the political, union, administrative and judicial spheres, even though, legally, women should face no discrimination. Current laws guarantee them the same access to education, employment, property, and decision-making spheres as men. The considerable gap between the legislation and the patriarchal reality of the Peul, Malinke or Susu societies, which make up the majority of the population and have contested central power for 40 years, is striking. Moreover, the rise of Islamic organizations – especially those with Wahhabi ideology – has had significant consequences on women's mode of dress and conduct. Women are increasingly seen wearing veils on the streets of Conakry. "Within households as well as in society at large, Guinean women remain subordinate to men, who wield power in almost all areas" (Bop 2000:20).

The movement of a greater number of women into political and administrative leadership continued with the establishment of Mali's Third Republic under Alpha Oumar Konaré in 1992, following a brief military transition.[9] This involved cabinet, parliamentary, administrative judicial, and diplomatic positions, traditionally held by men. Several women, including many academics, were appointed as ministers and ambassadors.[10] At the legislative elections in March 1992, their representation in the National Assembly was limited to 3 out of 129 deputies (2.3%), but by July 2002, it had increased to 15 out of 147 representatives (10.2%).

Despite the challenging political context, slogans advocating for women's access to citizenship and decision-making roles eventually struck a chord, even though entering these male-dominated political spaces was not without difficulties and suffering. Alongside this, the democratic transition that began in the 1990s led governments to co-opt women's issues.[11] This occurred as various conventions, initially adopted by African states during the Decade, were reaffirmed during the international conferences held in Beijing. Some nations used this shift to project a democratic image (Togo, Benin, Gambia), while others (Côte d'Ivoire, Nigeria, Senegal) changed their political direction. Meanwhile, countries engulfed in conflicts experienced total political destabilization, with their governing bodies becoming paralyzed.

The election results for female candidates in legislative elections between 1992 and 2002 reveal the slow pace of progress. The target rate of 25% female occupancy of parliamentary seats, which African women called for in the early years of the Decade, was not achieved in any West African country. At the same time, it was widely met in East and Southern Africa. As of March 31, 2004, data shows a female participation rate of 48.8% in Rwanda,[12] which surpasses Sweden (45.8%) by more than 3 points. This was followed by Mozambique (30%), South Africa (29.8%),[13] Namibia (26.4%) and Uganda (24.7%). For West Africa, Guinea and Senegal led with 19.3% and 19.2% of seats held by women, respectively. The average female participation in parliamentary bodies in sub-Saharan Africa was 14.2%, compared to 39.7% for Scandinavian countries and only about 18% for Europe (18.4%), the Americas (18.2%) and Asia (15%). It far exceeded the total for Arab countries, which have granted only 6% of legislative seats to women. It is worth noting that Mozambique appointed a female prime minister in February

2004, Luisa Dias Diogo, who holds a Ph.D. in development economics and had headed the Ministry of Economy, Finance and Planning since 1994.

In some countries, such as Benin and Cape Verde, the rate has remained stable. Over the past 10 years, the integration of women into Beninese politics has been significantly influenced by the increase in women with established careers, many of whom have backgrounds in law. As members of the judiciary, some of them participated in the national conference and supervised the elections. Benin also had a new First Lady, Rosine Soglo, whose husband was elected president after 17 years of military rule under General Mathieu. Like Nana Konadu Agyeman Rawlings, the equally active Rosine Soglo, a lawyer by profession, created a political party to support her husband's reelection. In the latest presidential elections, which saw the reelection of Kérékou and his return to civilian life, one of the candidates was a woman who, despite having received only a small share of the votes, nonetheless conducted a campaign that captured the attention of the wider population. Female candidates are exceptionally rare in other countries. For the region, the cases of the Ghanaian candidate Nana Konadu Agyeman Rawlings (1996), the Senegalese Marième Ly-Wone (2000) and the Mauritanian Aicha Mint Jeddan (2003) are worth noting. Indeed, throughout the rest of the continent, there have been no other candidates. In a rather surprising development in South Africa, President Thabo Mbeki dismissed his vice president, Jacob Zuma, who was accused of corruption. On June 22, 2005, he announced the appointment of the minister of minerals and energy, Phumzile Mlambo-Ngcuka, a grassroots organizer.

When Thomas Sankara and Bernard Compaoré, representing a new generation of leaders, took power in Burkina Faso in 1983, they were the first in the region to appoint women to key cabinet positions such as those overseeing the economy and budget. What was then called the revolution of Burkina Faso, the "pays des hommes intègres," aimed to combat the prevailing political corruption. Numerous laws were enacted in favor of women, in line with the demands of the time. After the military coup by Compaoré, during which Sankara was overthrown and killed, the discourse on women "cooled down." Administrative restructuring in 2000 led to the creation of a department for human rights, headed by a teacher from the Faculty of Law in Ouagadougou, known for her activism.

Despite efforts to promote women's rights, strengthened by the ongoing democratization of political regimes, female representation in political institutions remains low. Indeed, Togo, which had only one female deputy in 1992, now has six; but what role can they truly play in a parliament where the "legal" opposition is prohibited from taking seats?[14]

After enduring 15 years of military struggles, Liberia and Sierra Leone are now faced with the urgent tasks of restoring civic life and revitalizing their economy. However, new political programs are pervaded by concerns about women's issues, a direct result of the extensive violence (kidnappings, rapes, murders, assassinations) that women endured during the conflicts. The crisis, which originated in Liberia, spilled over into Sierra Leone and then Guinea due to the influx of refugees. In Sierra Leone, the political mobilization of women's organizations, created under various pretexts and united within the Sierra Leonean Association of NGOs (SLANGO), focused on addressing the issues stemming from the conflict.[15] These organizations have worked extensively to tackle the violence that occurred at that time. Their work is primarily concerned with collecting data and figures, gathering testimonies and supporting the victims of violence, including rape, domestic violence, sexual abuse and other human rights violations against women and children. They also work to support the Special Court for Sierra Leone established by the United Nations Security Council.

In Senegal, during the 40 years of Socialist Party rule, there were sweeping changes in the political landscape, with the decentralization policy initiated in 1972 taking a new turn with regionalization on January 1, 1997. In rural areas, rural representatives were generally appointed by the Socialist Party. However, these appointments seldom favored the promotion of women to leadership roles such as president, regional councilor or municipal councilor. Until the regional elections of 1997, only one woman had been elected president of a Rural Council. In 1990, rural representatives accounted for 5.6% of the total number of representatives across all 317 rural communities, and 15% of the total number of representatives in the 40 municipalities of the country before regionalization (Sow 1997). The regionalization of 1997 expanded this structure to involve 60 municipalities and 320 rural communities across 10 administrative regions, introducing substantial financial commitments. To support this expansion, the state established an Endowment Fund of about USD 8 million for its operation, which underscored the high stakes of the upcoming elections. The electoral performance of women for regional and municipal councilor positions remained steady, with their representation ranging between 13 and 15%. In March 2000, a democratic shift led to the ousting of the Socialist Party and the rise of a diverse coalition of opposition parties headed by the Parti démocratique sénégalais (PDS). The subsequent changes were significant. Notably, Mame Madior Boye took over as prime minister, marking the first time a woman held this position in both the country and the sub-region. Appointed in February 2001, she was confirmed in this role two months later, the day after the legislative elections that sealed the victory of the PDS. Although her powers were limited under the presidential system outlined by the new constitution, President Abdoulaye Wade's appointment of Boye – a non-partisan judge known for her integrity – served a dual purpose: acknowledging his female supporters and addressing a sensitive political situation.[16] Women were right to embrace this appointment as a significant shift in the attitudes of the average Senegalese man, validating that a woman not only could lead as prime minister but also was capable of holding any position. The prime minister's cabinet, formed in May 2001, included 5 women among its 25 ministers. Beyond handling traditional roles in social development and family affairs, these women also managed key departments such as health, decentralization, commerce, and small and medium-sized businesses. This number was close to that under the last Socialist government (1998–2000), which included 5 women out of 31 cabinet members, some of whom headed departments such as those of budget, communication and public service. The progress was clearer in the Parliament elected on April 29, 2001, where there were 21 women out of 120 deputies. During the previous legislature (1993–8), dominated by the Socialists, there were only 12 women out of 120. Barely two years into her tenure, the prime minister was ousted in a political reshuffle intended to position the government favorably for the upcoming legislative elections in 2006 and presidential elections in 2007. What should have been a victory for feminist struggles turned out to be just a tactical political move.

What can be said about the position of women in the ongoing battle among African political classes? Given the challenges of democratization, gender equality, social justice and respect for the individual that Africa faces, the core issue is the "imperative of meaningful representation" and the effective implementation of policies that are often launched in name only. This requires that women's power and their activities extend beyond mere folkloric representation, beyond formal quotas or official signs of parity. For decades, the presidential system of the one-party state has exploited the female electorate and the associative movement involved in economic, cultural, and religious activities for its own benefit. The feminist political project aimed to break away from this deceptive and unproductive manipulation. This is no easy feat, especially when considering women's involvement in a partisan landscape – driven by the pluralistic process of democratization – that fragments them.

A notable outcome of women's mobilization and gender debates was achieved during the establishment of the new African Union in Lusaka, Zambia, in July 2002. African heads of state decided to statutorily mandate a gender-balanced composition for the Commission responsible for managing the institution's activities, resulting in five of the ten commissioners being women. Following this commitment, and at least formally, the heads of state who signed the good governance observatory created a management committee for this initiative on a gender-parity basis. Moreover, in March 2004, they elected a woman to lead it.[17] These actions, while largely symbolic, send a strong signal about the impact of women's mobilization at decision-making and operational levels.

Securing appointments for women in high-ranking positions is only the first step forward. Despite most registered voters and those who turn out to vote being women, African parliamentarians are not yet elected on a gender-parity basis. Paradoxically, on a continent where the idea of female heads of state is not yet widely embraced, it might be more feasible to see women appointed by men in power to exceptional positions, such as prime minister or, more commonly, president of key judicial and constitutional bodies like the state council, supreme court or constitutional court. This has been the trend in countries like Senegal and Benin. Despite this progress, the male-dominated nature of the state still shows a preference for men holding positions of sovereignty, while appointing women based primarily on their professional competence and political loyalty.

1.4 The Status of Women as a Political Matter

Women's participation in the political sphere and their assumption of new responsibilities has been driven by questions concerning women's rights more than those concerning development, nation-building or societal projects. Since 1975, most African governments have gradually established structures to promote women's rights, while also signing favorable protocols, treaties and conventions, negotiated over the Decade. One achievement of these policies has been to make the conditions of women more visible politically, despite various obstacles. It was not within political parties that women brought these matters to the fore and discussed them, but rather within their various organizations. Before being integrated into what is now referred to as civil society, these organizations served as vital spaces for self-expression and freedom, allowing women to exercise and expand their understanding of citizenship. Women's organizations, rooted in a long tradition of women banding together around socio-cultural, political or economic interests, provided frameworks that governments, international organizations and NGOs used to deploy their supportive efforts, including professional associations, social clubs, women's groups and economic interest groups.

It wasn't until the years 1975–80 and the first global conferences on women that movements more focused on the everyday needs of women began to emerge. While men were fiercely criticizing the independence policies of a "Black Africa that had gotten off to a bad start,"[18] women started to focus on their daily hardships: the burden of domestic duties, barriers to education, high unemployment, the strain of high fertility rates, maternal mortality, as well as forced and early marriage, and the challenges of polygamy, along with the difficulty accessing political power. The priorities defined, the barriers denounced, the tone used, the level of commitment or conflict with the state, the party and other organizations varied depending on who was leading the organizing effort. Many instances have been identified where governments promoted what has been deemed "state feminism," using women's rights as a political tool rather than genuinely addressing the issues at hand. Co-optation by the wives of heads of state (the First Ladies syndrome), whose actions remain problematic, also must be mentioned.

Women have held responsibilities across several areas: politically (participating in governance), economically (engaging in economic activities – administration, education, entrepreneurship, and the so-called informal sector) and socially, particularly within the family (transforming their status within the family). The existing inequalities are reflected in everyday life. In heterogeneous societies shaped by custom or by Muslim or Judeo-Christian traditions, cultural factors play a crucial role as a reflection of social and religious norms. These cultural factors strongly influence women's efforts to articulate their legal and political rights and priorities. Women work against outdated perspectives to establish their economic objectives and define political strategies for their demands and actions. Cultural barriers, identity crises, and the struggles faced in everyday cultural and social life are magnified by the state's gender bias and patriarchal decision-making in both public and private sectors. These factors significantly heighten the obstacles women face in their demands for equality. We are witnessing a growing movement among women who are increasingly vocal in response to a survival-based economy that requires their greater involvement in managing both domestic duties and family finances.

The cultural aspect of this debate can be seen in broader initiatives that aim to reshape society by integrating universal values into societal and institutional frameworks. These efforts influence legislation and civil codes, especially in the area of family law. Following in the footsteps of many women's organizations, it is worth looking into issues such as the wearing of the veil, the confinement of women in polygamous "harems," their access to property or land-use rights, their rights in Muslim inheritance laws, the methods of inheriting assets from both parents, and issues around primogeniture. We might also take into consideration the increasingly restrictive religious arguments concerning women's rights to exert more legal authority within the family, and to control their bodies, sexuality and fertility.

The same major issues are at stake when it comes to respecting, preserving or returning to African culture. Positioning women's bodies as the site where cultural conflicts are expressed and contested, cultural fundamentalism stands as a counterpoint to religious fundamentalism. Criticism of women's attitudes and behaviors, which are seen as embodying the nation's cultural identity, is a central part of these discussions. Efforts to challenge cultural and religious violence – such as FGM, polygamy and *talaq*, or unilateral divorce at the husband's behest – are often viewed as an outright rejection of African culture before any real debate can even be had.

We might say that the demands of African women became feminist once they became centered on their own bodies. Today, it is commonplace to say that the body is the very site of women's oppression. But it took many years and countless debates for them to agree to frame the discussion in "sexual" terms. At 1980's World Conference on Women in Copenhagen, the African debate about women's bodies focused on fertility rather than sexuality. Feminist discourse on sexual freedom and birth control resonated less than discussions about risk-free motherhood in the face of alarming maternal mortality rates and the need for access to quality healthcare given the dire health situation. The issue of genital mutilation, which African women initially downplayed, eventually gained recognition as a form of violence against women. Today, there are concerns that the severity and mutilating nature of this practice are being softened by referring to it as "excision" or "cutting." It was acknowledging its violence that led to the enactment of laws. As for abortion, there is no serious debate around it. Infanticide, clearly not an ideal method of birth control, is frequently addressed in the courts of assize. Each time these courts convene, cases of infanticide are judged. Debates on contraception, particularly the use of condoms, are similar to those on abortion: they come and go depending on the prevailing political or religious ideology.

Re-evaluating women's roles within the family and challenging their "domestication" has been no easy task. This is primarily due to the domestic responsibilities and significant social role women play in managing social relations within the family and community. The family code, which few West African countries had in the 1960s, provided a critical entry point to question the family as an institutional system of gender inequalities. It also offered a key point of entry into the state's dual role in reinforcing these inequalities and protecting women, as well as the way Islamic and Christian religious patriarchies closely policed the expansion of women's freedoms. In West Africa, legal systems of French, British and Portuguese origin coexist, and these are in turn influenced by Islam and Christianity. To complicate matters further, all of this is built on a foundation of African cultures that still shape everyday social practices. These legal systems govern relationships within family models, which are themselves the subject of ideological and political power struggles. It is important to emphasize this mosaic of models rather than fall back on the illusion of a singular African family model.

The primary challenge of family law legislation centers on identity: how can laws rooted in Western and Judeo-Christian tradition be applied to the management of family, marriage, divorce and inheritance in different cultural contexts? This is reflected in the refusal or partial acceptance of colonial laws by Muslim communities, both before and after independence. In the colonial era, places such as Niger, Mali, Sierra Leone and Senegal drew on Sharia law in the framework of Muslim courts. Upon independence, Mali (1962), Guinea (1963), Senegal (1972), Cameroon (1981), Côte d'Ivoire (1983) and Burkina Faso (1990) introduced civil codes. After a few years, they reviewed and made improvements to these codes. Benin, which regulated marriage either by the Customary Law of Dahomey of 1931 or by the French Civil Code of 1958, did not adopt its own law until June 2002. Neither Niger nor Chad proposed laws specific to their communities, which had only the choice between Sharia law and the old French Civil Code inherited from colonization. Mauritania reverted to Sharia law in the early 1970s when the mixed African–Arab government opted for the status of an Islamic Republic to affirm its ties to the Arab world.

Another challenge is both religious and political, as demonstrated by the rejection by Islamic organizations of these secular codes at the time of their drafting. What was a religious stance in the 1960s and 1970s has taken on an increasingly political dimension with the resurgence of Islamic movements in the 1980s and the growth of fundamentalism in the 1990s. Several organizations in Muslim countries have sought to re-evaluate the family codes and challenged the legal gains afforded by secularism, particularly the celebration or registration of marriage in civil offices, the requirement for expressed consent from spouses themselves, judicially handled divorces and the legal determination of alimony.

Debates about the family led African feminists to organize into advocacy groups that eventually succeeded in getting an additional protocol on women's rights added to the African Charter on Human and Peoples' Rights. While they failed in abolishing polygamy in their national family codes or in legalizing abortion, they managed to include these issues in the Charter through discussions with national experts, ministers and heads of state at the African Union summit in July 2003.

1.5 Conclusion

Understanding and measuring women's political mobilization remains a challenge in the current context. For men, this mobilization is generally measured in terms of participation in political parties and power, involvement in governmental programs, and campaign promises aimed at securing citizenship rights as defined by constitutions, laws and other development goals focused on growth. The approach is more complex for women, due to the patriarchal and male-dominated nature of the state and the political sphere. Despite the new perspectives introduced by political practices from the colonial era and efforts at social modernization, these changes have not fully ended the marginalization of women in countries where they remain largely unacknowledged as full citizens. Though there are many obstacles barring them from the political arena, women have created their own spaces for expression and autonomy by participating in liberation struggles and supporting men in power, but have yet to be adequately acknowledged or compensated for their efforts.

If women's organizations have been given so much attention, it is because they have been privileged spaces for women to speak out and take political action. Recent literature has discussed the "theatricalization" of political power in contemporary Africa. Women are both "spectators" and "ushers" in this theater, from which they gain less for their rights than they do from women's organizations, which range from economic interest groups and *mbootaay* to friendly societies and associations of various natures. These organizations have given them a platform for self-expression and encouraged them to continue to fight for their rights, including in battles that they have won. Issues like access to land, credit and technology, the abolition of FGM, the right to contraception, parental authority, the education of girls, and the ability to participate in decision-making have been addressed and advocated for by these organizations, not by political parties – even those on the left. Parties only pay lip service to women's demands, which include opposing the application of Sharia law, abolishing polygamy and condemning physical violence, abuse and sexual harassment, as well as supporting political quotas or parity.

However, their struggle remains difficult due to discriminatory practices and class constraints that women either endure or embody themselves. They often internalize the relationships of inequality between men and women reinforced by family, culture, law or religion. As many have noted, even within administrative or parliamentary bureaucracies, women continue to experience male domination or use its forms and terms to gain power.

The discussions from the Decade have helped to solidify the discourse on gender equality and the empowerment of women. Ten years after Beijing, in the current context of economic globalization and the rise of religious and political fundamentalisms, the achievements of women are under threat. They are called into question by international institutions and aid organizations that have contributed to bolstering women's aspirations for freedom. This regression is intolerable. Only political mobilization can prevent it. And we must create the means for that to take place.

2

Appropriation of Gender Studies in Sub-Saharan Africa (2007)[1]

In the 1970s, discussions on gender and social relations between men and women initially caught the African social science research community off guard. This community was active and vibrant, yet it focused on other issues it deemed more critical at the time. Following the decolonial era, their main concerns were directly tied to the aftermath of colonization and the need to establish a stable independence. Their focus was largely on development, cultural revival, state-building, national unity, addressing neocolonialism and redefining political power. This led to a "politically correct" mindset where issues concerning women and gender relations were seen as secondary or even trivial. It took time for feminist issues to be recognized as a legitimate area of academic inquiry, only emerging toward the end of the 1970s. However, by the early 2000s, there was a clear recognition of the importance of women's issues and gender relations, despite some remaining controversies. This progress was highlighted by an international conference in Abidjan titled "Gender, Population, and Development in Africa," which attracted many researchers from different nationalities and fields, and which was supported by academic and governmental institutions. This event exemplified the strides made and helped promote a supportive environment for integrating this new disciplinary field into the social sciences across Africa.

The United Nations Decade for Women (1975–85), along with the follow-up assessments in Beijing in 1995,[2] played a crucial role in raising global awareness about feminist concerns and shaping discussions on gender roles. In Africa, the creation of Women's Bureaus and ministries dedicated to women's issues, as well as numerous women's organizations and non-governmental organizations (NGOs), provided these debates with an institutional framework. Various conferences and events have effectively informed public opinion and engaged political leaders on these issues (awareness campaigns in urban and rural areas, across media platforms including radio, television and the press).

Early academic research on feminist issues largely reproduced the intellectual work that women were already carrying out on the ground. Various groups, including women's associations, feminist NGOs, international organizations and African governments, tackled these issues with mixed results, which further highlights their complex implications. They adapted ideas and language to suit their purposes and pace amidst local, national and international pressures. They disseminated, modified, distorted or even rejected feminist concerns. At times, they opted to address these issues on an African timescale (i.e., postponing them indefinitely), while waiting for a natural and "endogenous" evolution in cultural attitudes and mindsets. Despite these challenges, a meaningful discourse on women and gender emerged, warranting thorough analysis.

Rather than dwelling on the definitions of concepts related to women and gender, my focus will be on the challenges of deploying these concepts as analytical tools within the mainstream of African social sciences. Mainstreaming gender has had only relative success, as it is met sometimes with ignorance or indifference, and other times with acceptance or resistance (Sow 1995; Mama 1996). Despite this wavering of public opinion, there is no shortage of studies on women in every context (women and health, women and employment, entrepreneurship, politics, environment, human rights, globalization, and so on). Most of these studies are conducted by women and a few "courageous" men. It is worth examining the controversies these studies have sparked concerning women's issues and approaches to the question of gender. This entails assessing the shared concerns, conflicts and contradictions faced by African women, caught between the pressures of feminist activism aimed at addressing the challenges affecting women and the requirements of objective scientific analysis. At the same time, we must not overlook the fact that any claim on the universality of feminist thought is valid only if it encompasses all cultural models. Citing "cultural relativism" as a static value system in non-Western societies misleadingly assumes the West is the only benchmark. While recognizing the successes and failures of a gender-centric approach, it is crucial to maintain its interdisciplinary reach and applicability, which spans fields from history to medicine and from agriculture to political or religious studies.

2.1 Gender Discourse: Forms of Resistance and Compromise

In the context of development, women's and gender studies continue to encounter strong resistance, even within academic circles. As a form of backlash, many men have adopted various postures of "machismo," which range from polite disdain to outright dismissal. And when these approaches become popular, they are quick to co-opt them. Everyone engaged in feminist research or activism can share experiences of being on the receiving end of sarcastic or even hostile comments from friends, acquaintances and colleagues regarding women's and gender studies, reflecting a deep-seated animosity.

At the close of an international symposium held in Dakar in May 1999, filled with multidisciplinary debates on francophone feminist research, a prominent Senegalese historian sharply criticized the discussions: "This debate misses the point! Girls today are free because they are prostituting themselves to foreign tourists and making advances on married men!" In a session discussing the relevance of gender studies for future African research, one irritated participant dismissed the feminist approach as "overly reliant on foreign perspectives and irrelevant to African culture, which holds women in high regard!" Another, speaking sarcastically, tellingly remarked, "My colleague claims she enjoys cooking dinner for her family herself after a day at the office."

For some, the reluctance to engage in these discussions stems from the belief that gender relations in Africa do not follow a culturally defined hierarchy, or that biological differences "naturally" justify (and thus legitimize) inequalities between men and women. For others, the reasons are quite different. Mainstreaming gender goes beyond just reforming or broadening our understanding; it challenges the very legitimacy of how empirical knowledge is produced – questioning who produces it, in what manner, for whom, and for what purpose. These conflicts are not unique to issues of women and gender. As Ayesha Imam highlights, "Every theoretical and methodological framework of knowledge production has implicit values and assumptions about the nature of society and will be resisted by those who do not have the same position" (1997:16). The stakes of debates on African history, languages and imperialism, pursued under the banner of decolonizing the social sciences, have been immense. With similar ambition, examining and accepting gender differences and relations as an analytic tool reveals how these differences perpetuate inequalities and underscore the contingent nature of male privileges. This examination is often met with (predominantly male) hostility because it challenges male dominance and privileges, even questioning the very assumptions on which masculinity rests. Feminist thought is frequently dismissed as ideological, excessively influenced by foreign views, and lacking in analytical rigor to undermine its credibility and suppress its voice.

While these sarcastic attacks might appear shocking, they are even more startling when they come from established female scholars. Even though they align with feminist ideologies, these women challenge the "universality" of such views and often rightly distrust the logic and contributions of Western women. For example, a Malian sociologist once criticized me for having a "victim mentality" when I pointed out, during a conference on security in African cities,[3] the heightened vulnerability of women to various types of violence, both in public and at home. She argued that this perspective unfairly portrays men and African society negatively, at a time when there is already so much Afro-pessimism.

Over two decades of debates concerning women's status, roles, rights and targeted capacity-building initiatives have led to widespread awareness in Africa of discrimination against women. Concepts such as subordination, oppression, patriarchal power, emancipation, liberation, parity and human rights have gradually become part of the discursive field of and about women. Yet these concepts have only been incorporated into mainstream thought to the extent that they do not radically alter the established order[4] or fundamentally challenge existing power dynamics or sociocultural identities, which are fraught with contradictions and disparities. Religion often reinforces these identity-centric arguments. It took nearly two decades for several African parliaments to approve the abolition of female genital mutilation (FGM), which was resisted because it attacked core cultural values that define "true" feminine identity. For some Muslim communities, FGM was considered a religious practice to ensure women's purity.[5] In response, some groups even proposed alternative rituals to replace FGM. Women's organizations could only publicly oppose FGM by framing it as a medical issue and linking it to other harmful practices affecting maternity and child health, such as force-feeding, early marriage and traditional childbirth methods.[6] The profound implications for women's sexual rights and bodily integrity that result from FGM were only emphasized much later.[7]

The acceptance of women's and gender issues is quite mixed across society, academic circles, government and even international organizations (which fund programs that support women), often resulting in significant compromises. In terms of women's rights, concessions are frequently granted to women without a genuine commitment to implement them. Numerous local and international women's groups have taken a stand for these rights, supported by both popular and academic literature, media campaigns and advocacy efforts. Despite official declarations promoting women's liberation, empowerment and advancement, women continue to contend with the constraints of male dominance and enduring prejudices regarding their supposed inferiority. The international agreements designed to protect these rights, although ratified by governments, are seldom enforced, leading to ongoing compromises in the battle against gender inequality and precarious living conditions.

2.2 Feminism: Questions, Convictions and Ambivalences in Africa

During the 1960s, as feminism experienced revival alongside other social movements, it challenged the dominant patriarchal order and advocated for equal rights and status. However, women in sub-Saharan Africa had other priorities that often overshadowed their conditions as women. Active in movements against colonial rule, they initially lent their support to the brothers and later the fathers of the independence movements. Their cause as women was lost during this involvement, a phenomenon observed by Stephanie Urdang (1989) in her study of liberation movements in Mozambique – a trend also evident in other movements such as the West African RDA (Rassemblement Démocratique Africain), the Algerian FLN (Front de Libération Nationale) and the PAIGC of Guinea-Bissau and the Cape Verde Islands (Partido Africano da Independência da Guiné e Cabo Verde). Although women actively participated in various forms of political and armed resistance, they were often excluded from leadership roles and relegated to domestic life after the conflicts ended.

Despite the establishment of increasingly influential women's organizations during the colonial period, the nationalist cause remained the top priority. African women opposed colonial political and economic control by supporting movements organized by men, such as the strike of railway workers' wives in Thiès, Senegal, in 1946 (Sembène 1960).[8] Additionally, they fought for legitimate labor rights, which primarily concerned men. For example, trader organizations in the Gulf of Benin countries – Dahomey, Togo, Nigeria and Ghana – protested against the high taxes, licenses and other fees imposed by colonial authorities. They also highlighted issues such as inadequate working conditions, poor hygiene and healthcare, and limited access to education, especially for adults (Akpaki 2001).

In the 1950s and at the dawn of the decolonial era, various women's movements supported the efforts of political figures such as Kwame Nkrumah in Ghana and Sylvanius Olympio in Togo. However, these movements rarely challenged the restrictive conditions imposed on women by local cultures, which were often overtly patriarchal or shaped by the patriarchal norms of colonial regimes and Abrahamic religions. Discussions about the dynamics between men and women avoided critical scrutiny, as these dynamics were perceived mainly as "complementary." Addressing gender issues was often seen as irrelevant, deemed a concern only for Western feminists who were grappling with contradictions specific to their cultures. African women were instead encouraged to focus on liberation and the development of the continent. As independent African nations confronted the complexities and setbacks of nation-building, it was claimed that they could not afford to engage in debates about political and ethnic differences, let alone sexual differences. In the name of national and pan-African unity, many other differences were either obscured or forcefully suppressed.

It wasn't until between 1975 and 1980, during the first global women's conferences, that movements advocating for more personal rights began to emerge. While men focused exclusively on attacking the policies from the era of independence – a period often referred to saying "L'Afrique noire est mal partie" ["Black Africa got off to a bad start"] (Dumont 1962)[9] – women started to draw attention to their daily struggles: heavy domestic responsibilities, limited education or unemployment, challenging fertility issues, high maternal mortality, as well as forced and early marriages, and polygamy. They maintained a generally moderate tone, aiming not to echo the old colonial ethnological stereotypes of the African woman as a slave and beast of burden, and they remained hopeful that true independence and economic growth would alleviate their problems.

Feminism under Scrutiny

To be sure, feminist discourse was not immediately embraced. Right from the start at the first United Nations conferences on women during the 1970s, it was sharply criticized for its perceived "arrogance" and lack of sensitivity to the diverse national contexts and women's varying living conditions. Few African women self-identified as feminists. Westerners, especially Americans, had created the theoretical frameworks, concepts and strategies based on their unique histories and experiences, with figures such as Betty Friedan (1963) and Kate Millet (1971) being among the most notable. Their approach often promoted a universalist perspective on women's issues, demands and tactics while overlooking the realities faced by women in other continents. In North America and beyond, female activists from different races and classes spoke out against these universalist claims. This opposition is best expressed in works by Americans such as bell hooks in *Ain't I a Woman: Black Women and Feminism* (1981), Patricia Hill Collins in *Black Feminist Thought* (1990), and the British Hazel Carby in "White Woman Listen! Black Feminism and the Boundaries of Sisterhood" (1982), all of whom are of African or Caribbean descent. They argued that focusing solely on sex and gender was an oversimplification, and that race, nationality and class played a more significant role in the discrimination against women of color in America.

This "arrogance," consistently criticized by women from the Global South (Mernissi 1984),[10] arises from the dominant role of institutionalized feminist research in American universities, particularly within women's studies – and, later, gender studies – departments. This scholarly work, which is well funded and well represented, influences discussions globally, affecting North America, Europe, Latin America, the Caribbean, Asia and Africa. Despite its distinct approach, it still functions as an extension of traditional academic research.

Anglophone feminist thought, having already incorporated the categories of sex and gender into its theoretical framework, turned its attention to the status, roles and living conditions of women in the postcolonial Third World. This shift occurred within the field of development studies, leading to a substantial body of literature that introduced theoretical approaches and analytical tools such as WID (Women in Development), WAD (Women and Development) and GAD (Gender and Development). At that time, staging these struggles within an international context and seeking solutions and alliances at that scale had not yet taken off. Like their counterparts in other North American communities, African women challenged the prevailing male–female binary and the influence of the patriarchy, pointing to the impacts of colonialism, imperialism, the international division of labor, and unequal exchange on women's lives. They strongly criticized the tendency to lump women into categories like "Third World," "underdeveloped" and "Global South," and debated the priorities for reflection and action. Amidst these struggles, African women's organizations sought to carve out their own path, which was to be distinct from American and European women's liberation movements. In 1976, a group of African academics[11] attending a conference on "Women and National Development" at Wellesley College in the USA chose to form their own group and, the following year in Dakar, they founded the Association of African Women for Research and Development (AAWORD). This was the first continent-wide association focusing on women and development, connecting researchers and activists from Algiers to Cape Town across various disciplines and languages.

From the outset, non-African members were explicitly excluded. The inaugural meeting in 1977 centered on decolonizing research. Although most members were, and continue to be, academics, AAWORD, based in Dakar, conducts its research independently of universities.

Rethinking Women's Issues from an African Cultural Perspective
It is helpful to present here a few key debates concerning feminist theories and approaches in relation to African culture. Three theoretical approaches stand out from recent texts that draw and expand on current trends of African research. They stem from the work of Oyèrónké Oyéwùmí (1997), Saliou Kanji and Fatou-Kiné Camara (2000) and Ndri Assié-Lumumba (1996), respectively.

The first approach can be found in Oyèrónké Oyéwùmí's *The Invention of Women: Making an African Sense of Western Gender Discourses* (1997).[12] This work represents a radical rejection of feminism, including its analytical tools and methods. The Nigerian sociologist criticizes, in the name of African cultural specificity, what she terms the "invention of women" by Western feminists. Right off the bat, in the preface, she challenges the relevance of their "imperialist" gender discourse to African societies, arguing that the Western focus on biological differences as a fundamental social determinant does not align with African realities. According to Oyéwùmí, the construction of the category of "woman," defined in relation to the body and positioned in contrast to the category of "man," does not exist in pre-colonial Yoruba society. She contends that this dichotomy is a colonial legacy, as hierarchies in Yoruba society were not based on sex but on social relationships. Unlike the West, where biology shapes social ideology and roles, Yoruba society does not consider an individual's anatomy as defining their social status (1997:13). Moreover, she asserts that there is no gendered cultural logic – that is, a cultural logic based on sexual division – in Yoruba society. She critiques Western concepts such as man, woman and patriarchy, which she argues are based on fundamentally "bio-logical" rationalizations, and claims they are a "Western parody" of universality (1997:176). These constructs, she argues, are inapplicable to Yoruba society, where social categories do not hinge on anatomical differences.

To support her argument, Oyèrónké Oyéwùmí cites several examples. One such example is the concept of seniority, where relationships between elders and youth play a more critical role in determining power dynamics among individuals than gender does. Another example is motherhood, which she presents as foundational to women's power because it is central to their identity. Oyéwùmí criticizes the misguided application of Western experiences as universally relevant and concludes: "African feminists can learn a lot from the methods of feminist scholarship as they have been applied to the West, but they should scorn methods of Western, imperial, feminist Africanists who impose feminism on the 'colonies.' African scholars need to do serious work detailing and describing indigenous African cultures from the inside out, not from the outside in" (1997:21).

Any approach that frames gender issues within a divisive and antagonistic male/female binary tends to pathologize women globally (1997:178). This perspective can hinder the understanding of women's issues and influence the development of policies that affect them. Saliou Kanji and Fatou-Kiné Camara (2000) arrive at the same conclusion regarding the misguided – not to say irrelevant – application of gender as a conceptual category and the underlying assumption of women's subordinate position. They explore this idea with analytical rigor and precision in their book *L'union matrimoniale dans la tradition des peuples noirs*.

This critique also targets the Western cultural tendency to universalize principles such as male dominance, female subordination and the superiority of their models of human rights. Describing the universal subordination of women as a "stereotype," the authors boldly state in their introduction that "Black law is fundamentally feminist" (2000:19). They explain that Black law draws upon a "Black civilization spanning from ancient Egypt to pre-colonial sub-Saharan Africa, and across the global African diaspora, including the Caribbean, the Americas, and even the Dravidians of India" (2000:11). Rooted in pharaonic law, which serves as the foundation for many Black cultures, this system is based on matriarchy, which assumes equality between men and women – a core value of pharaonic society. This perspective is also adopted by the work of Egyptologist Christine Desroches-Noblecourt, who observes that Egyptian women retained full legal rights upon marriage or motherhood (1986:171). Christian Jacq (1996) highlights the unparalleled freedom and power of Egyptian women compared to Greek women, a level of autonomy that many modern Western women would envy. Saliou Kanji and Fatou-Kiné Camara observe these principles of law and equality reflected in the culture, legal practices and languages of predominantly African societies inspired by Black-Egyptian heritage. For example, both Wolof (2000:19) and Yoruba (Oyéwùmí 1997:33) languages have unique terms to describe a person (*nit, èníyàn*), a woman (*jigeen, obìnrin*) and a man (*goor, okùnrin*), emphasizing biological differences without implying inequality. Unlike the English terms "human," "man" and "woman," these African terms neither suggest superiority nor inferiority. Moreover, "in the same spirit of gender equality, gender distinctions are eliminated in adjectives, articles, and possessive pronouns, eliminating any notion of derogatory femininity or exclusionary masculinity" (2000:20). Matriarchy, pivotal to Black civilization, emphasizes the feminine principle as a source of life and power without creating a system of inequality. The authors draw from the seminal work of Cheikh Anta Diop (1959) who explains that:

> matriarchy does not signify the absolute or cynical dominance of women over men; instead, it embodies a harmonious balance – a mutual agreement between the sexes aimed at building a stable society where each individual flourishes by performing roles best suited to their physical nature. This matriarchal system is not forced upon men by unavoidable circumstances; rather, it is willingly accepted and actively supported by them. (1959:114)

This "feminism" inherent in "Black" law, then, affords women significant respect and freedom within the framework of marital law. Here, celibacy is a right; entering into marriage is a voluntary decision that does not define a woman's status; choosing a partner is entirely free, sometimes with preferred clauses; marital residence is typically near the woman's home (*uxorilocal*); a dowry does not signify purchasing a bride but is a symbol of alliance and acknowledgment; and sexual union is seen as a contract for mutual assistance. The authors ultimately assert that, while this system may appear to place men in a seemingly inferior role, they do not suffer from this arrangement because, at its core, marriage is considered a partnership agreement.

Continuing the call to restore the historical values of Black cultures and to "decolonize" research and its conceptual frameworks, Ndri Assié-Lumumba, in her 2000 article "Le genre dans la recherche en Afrique" ("Gender in African Research"), criticizes "the denial of Africans' historical experiences [which] translates to a rejection or non-recognition of their experiences in the specific area of gender relations." She continues:

Paradoxically, at a time when Westerners have started to recognize that Africans have a rich history, and that culture and civilization are aspects of all human experiences, including those of Africans, the discourse on gender and the status of African women in their societies are often framed as if they must necessarily conform to Western intellectual approaches, particularly those of Western feminism. Thus, moving from the depiction by nineteenth and early twentieth century missionaries and anthropologists of African societies as "primitive," where women were viewed as mere beasts of burden, we now consider the experiences of African women as part of the global narrative of women's exploitation by men. (2000:13)

Ndri Assié-Lumumba emphasizes the significant contributions of women in African history and culture to economic, social and scientific advances, as well as to forms of governance. Drawing from the critiques of Western feminism by African (Filomena Chioma Steady 1981) and African American (Terborg-Penn et al. 1987) feminists, she points to the pre-colonial Baoulé women as an example to introduce the concepts of "parallel autonomy" and "positive, empowering, and dynamic complementarity" between men and women. In these societies, men and women operate in distinct social spaces, performing activities and responsibilities that are individually or collectively managed and are generally complementary or even equal. For instance, during funerals, while men are responsible for burial rituals, women manage all the social aspects surrounding death, such as hosting guests, accepting condolences, exchanging gifts and performing rituals for the deceased. However, unlike previous writers on these issues, Ndri Assié-Lumumba values the integration of a gender-centric perspective, arguing that it exposes social contradictions and inequalities, providing a deeper understanding of the lived experiences of both men and women.

These various engagements and critiques of feminist theories are part of a broader movement of decolonization and reinterpretation led by African women themselves. They aim to reclaim what they view as overlooked historical truths and cultural specificities. This effort to reframe sociology, culture and history can be surprising and even provocative, as it takes on significant ideological, scientific, political, economic and methodological matters. African women strive to analyze their societies with rigor and integrity, drawing on concepts that mirror their realities while avoiding oversimplification and careless generalizations taken from different contexts.

This concern leads to the conclusions presented here, based on a selective literature review that questions the reliability of using gender as a universal analytical tool across all societies. These writers challenge the universality of the concepts of gender relations underpinning feminist thought, which are deeply embedded in specific sociohistorical contexts. While recognizing these contexts is crucial, it is also necessary to confront the real social differences between genders and the power dynamics within relationships. Research must establish frameworks and conditions that mobilize efforts to dismantle inequitable relations. In response to the arguments outlined above, we would do well to cite many critiques, especially that of Bibi Bakare-Yusuf, who provides a well-argued counterpoint to Oyèrónké Oyéwùmí's perspective.

It should be clear, then, that the methodological and conceptual framework used to study women in Africa is of utmost importance. Researchers in Africa (and elsewhere) must critically examine the tools used to conceptualize ideas and sociocultural practices, especially those formulated in the indigenous languages of the societies being studied. Socialization occurs through various codes shaped by culture, education, religion, among other factors, which are transmitted through language from one person to another, across groups and generations. Hence, understanding languages and their symbolism is crucial to fully grasp the nuances of a society. Titi Ufomata adds further support to this idea, arguing that:

> Language is therefore a medium of culture. The relationship between language and culture is dynamic and symbiotic. Languages reflect communities just as communities impact languages. Thus, if one operates in a linguistic system in which a husband is referred to as "master" (*oga* in Nigerian pidgin English) and one accepts the

terms and its connotations unquestioningly, then consciously or unconsciously one accepts the power relations subsumed in its usage. (1998:62)

Ufomata, while taking a more moderate approach in respect to Oyèrónké Oyéwùmí's claims, agrees that language critically shapes cultural values, but emphasizes the need to examine its transformations on the level of both form and substance, arguing that "a more accurate account of words that conveys meaning across time would be one that emphasizes flux rather than stasis and conservation." Understanding the situation of women also means studying their history. Such an analysis must remain dynamic, lest it fall into cultural determinism or essentialism. While values and the terms that describe them are indeed culturally specific, they are not immutable; they evolve through time and space, changing the representations and meanings associated with them. This approach allows us to critically reassess dominant views on women's conditions by examining historical contexts and reflecting on various transformations up to the present.

The concept of seniority, as explored by Oyèrónké Oyéwùmí, is a widespread social phenomenon in which relationships between elders and youth are expressed as forms of subordination.[13] This dynamic confers moral and social standing to both women and men across many modern African societies. In these contexts, older women often have authority over younger men, while older men have authority over younger women, especially their wives and daughters. According to Oyèrónké Oyéwùmí, in the realm of marriage – a critical sphere for gender relations – these interactions are influenced by seniority. But as Bibi Bakare-Yusuf notes, seniority inherently involves power dynamics, regardless of gender. The head of a family wields significant authority, establishing hierarchical and dominant relationships. Contemporary sociology studies the family in light of its internal dynamics, arrangements, disputes, negotiations and conflicts among individuals, regardless of their gender. This view was already embedded in Wolof family norms, which advise new spouses about the inherent conflicts in marriage and encourage mutual patience.

In discussing polygamy, Kanji and Camara describe a system where the first wife (*aawo*) holds a superior status, not unlike a "governor" supported by additional wives who are not meant to replace her but to assist and support her in her role (2000:173). Although this arrangement supposedly elevates the first wife, it raises questions about the subordinate position of the other wives. What power do the subsequent wives hold? Did they enter into a polygamous relationship in order to support and assist the first wife? Or was it to lighten their heavy domestic burdens, which traditionally fall only on women due to societal norms? This arrangement prompts a deeper inquiry into whether these responsibilities are inherently female or a result of patriarchal ideologies. We could equally challenge the idealized image of motherhood as a symbol of feminine power, even as something almost divine – a view upheld by some African thinkers like Ifi Amadiume (1997) and Oyèrónké Oyéwùmí (2000). While motherhood undeniably plays a key role in determining women's social status, the idea of not being a mother remains deeply problematic. Have women really had the power to decide how many children to have – or whether to have children at all? Have we made any progress on this? We cannot ignore the current debates around the patriarchal and nationalist ideologies that underlie the glorification of motherhood. As central as motherhood is to many women's lives, it can also "easily become a trap" (McFadden 1997:1).

This raises questions regarding similar issues, such as spouse selection, the implications of dowries, or non-judicial divorces – areas where women often lack social control. Forced marriages persist, affecting in particular very young girls. Dowries are never negotiated by the bride herself. In Muslim contexts, while men can unilaterally initiate a divorce, women must negotiate with their families to proceed. In the 1980s, during debates on the discrimination faced by women in developing countries, the family was described as a space of "domestication" for women (Rogers 1980).

Countless studies on African culture show how deeply internal changes have reshaped social systems and cultural values, the influence of Muslim and Judeo-Christian religions, and both colonial and modern Western models, which speaks to the need to re-evaluate social relations between individuals, including men and women.[14] This re-evaluation must consider the multiple changes that have occurred. Although differences between men and women do not inherently lead to inequality in all cases, the

pervasive inequalities and gender-based discriminations reported
by African women are undeniable. The notion of the feminization
of poverty extends beyond feminist discourse. The concept of
equality in civil rights and the rights of children, while rooted in
a distinctly Western experience, may demand cautious consideration, but it stands as a universal principle despite international
differences. The idea of role complementarity between genders
does not amount to true equality. Women's interests lie not in the
conditional citizenship defined by ancient Greek society but in a
full, democratic citizenship envisioned in the new millennium.

2.3 African Feminist Thought: What Purpose Does It Serve?

Contributions of African Research
The numerous debates and conferences on feminism held around
the world have affirmed the international importance of these
issues. Clearly, African women could not remain excluded
from debates directly involving them as subjects from former
colonies, the Third World, developing countries and the Global
South. African research asserts, first and foremost, the right to
speak, the right to tell and write its own story, and to debate
its identity in terms reflective of its own experiences. What has
long been acknowledged in the Global North has taken time to
gain recognition in the Global South and other developing areas.
The dominant ideologies of the Global North have been slow to
recognize the emergence and validity of perspectives from the
Global South.

African feminist thought offers three major contributions,
which it should prioritize. First, it should expose the complex
situations of women by examining how factors like gender,
race, class, religion and caste contribute to their experiences.
Second, it should enhance the field by refining and expanding
the concepts and methodologies that contribute to a broader
universal understanding. Lastly, it is of utmost importance to
convince both the African academic community and the general
public of the vital importance and relevance of feminist discourse
in advancing women's causes.

Just as Western research explores history to understand the
present without confining it within rigid boundaries, African

research must also navigate this route without succumbing to an exotic form of anthropology that restricts specific topics to certain experts. Anthropological approaches have often placed dynamic social realities into fixed categories under the banner of "alterity," a notion that is fortunately challenged today, despite persistent resistance. Kabyle, Hal Pulaar or Tutsi women have been "fossilized" by ethno-anthropology. It is critical to dismantle sexist and racist prejudices that exacerbate the marginalization of women. Colonial and developmental policies have failed to grant women the autonomy they were promised. Income-generating activities and microcredit schemes have leveraged their labor for community development without providing them with substantial benefits.

African women are reclaiming their history both to challenge the assumed universal approach to women's issues that has overlooked their unique experiences and to affirm their legitimacy against criticisms of adopting Western perspectives from their African peers. This explains why they are fighting to have their distinct differences and priorities recognized. However, in the process, some have unintentionally contributed to the "fossilization" of cultural values and the roles of women, as discussed above. This issue was raised by French feminists at the 1972 Society for African Culture conference in Abidjan, which focused on "The Civilization of Women in African Traditions." The proceedings were published under the same title by Présence africaine (*La civilisation de la femme dans la tradition africaine*). These feminists were unconvinced by the portrayal of women's exceptional contributions to African society as described by the participants. Although the participants sought to prop up their argument with ample support, feminists pointed to its overarching theoretical flaws. In its 1987 publication, titled *La femme noire dans la vie moderne, images et réalités* (*The Black Woman in Modern Life, Images and Realities*), Présence africaine aimed to address these flaws.

Beyond the right to speak, being part of African culture offers a deeper perspective from within, making it essential to explore historical legacies to inform, report and reconstruct identities of alterity. The scholarly work of documenting languages, written and oral literatures, traditions, objects and cultural symbols is vital for understanding any society. We cannot grasp the current situation of women without examining their historical contexts, which must be studied with the analytical frameworks and critical tools that have been honed over time. Discussions on polygamy can be reframed by viewing marital relationships through different emotional and relational lenses. Polygamy involves more than just distributing women around a single husband – it also encompasses complex emotional dynamics involving jealousy, anger and aggression. For instance, as women enter menopause and gain status as revered "ancestors," potentially assuming political roles, their sexual relationships may wane, leading their husbands to seek younger partners or extra-marital affairs.

Many scholars, such as Filomena Chioma Steady, highlight unique practices within Africa, noting that institutions like female marriage to other women and the sexual ambiguity of some deities challenge Western binary models (Steady 2005:316). For example, Steady references Ifi Amadiume's influential 1997 book, *Male Daughters, Female Husbands*, which explores these symbolic customs and their profound meanings. But these representations are neither universal nor commonly found across Africa – nor are they broadly applicable in today's context. To be sure, they do not reflect the daily experiences of most women, nor do women in the West or East base their present and future on mythical or exceptional figures. This "selective" or "reified" history does not do justice to either women or science. In their study on the status of women in pre-colonial Africa, Achola Pala and Madina Ly (1979) stress the importance of analyzing these distinct practices within their historical context.

It is important, then, that African feminist research contribute to the discourse on universality by drawing from the continent's diverse cultural and historical human experiences. While framing feminist questions within the context of cultural relativism can risk overlooking shared challenges related to women's freedoms, it is crucial that each region contributes uniquely to developing the field. This approach helps bridge the Global North/South divide, focusing not on forced consensus or superficial solidarity but on thoughtful dialogue about shared concerns. Feminists from both the Global North and South find common ground in addressing widespread gender discrimination and the severe challenges women face across different cultures, even as they adapt their strategies to specific local contexts and priorities.

Make no mistake, there are cultural divides between women from the Global North and the Global South, but sometimes these lines blur when certain practices, despite their "exotic" appearance, have similar consequences. FGM is a prime example; it is not unique to African societies. Western feminists have pointed out that, even up to the 1950s, some medical practitioners performed surgeries that mutilated women's genitals under the guise of restoring these women to a "normal" life. Specifically, clitoridectomy or clitoral reduction was performed to prevent masturbation among girls. Similarly, tolerating polygamy or the wearing of the Islamic veil in the name of cultural relativism when practiced by communities from the Global South, while condemning these practices in the Global North, turns a blind eye to fundamental feminist issues regarding women's rights, bodily integrity and freedom.[15] Fundamentalism, arising from all belief systems, poses threats to women. Whether it is Christian groups attacking abortion clinics, Islamist militants enforcing "temporary marriages" through kidnapping, or qadis in northern Nigeria threatening women with death for adultery, these actions are abuses of women's bodies in the name of their respective faith.

The third key contribution of African feminist research should be to persuade the scientific community, both men and women, to embrace the diverse theories and methodologies that have demonstrated their effectiveness in Africa and globally. One might ask, "Who fears feminism?" – especially given the substantial impact that gender-centric conceptualizations and methodologies have had.

Over the past three decades of debates over women's issues, African women have forged their own understanding of issues such as development, modernization, technological advancement, the international division of labor, and the global economic order. They have engaged in discussions with women globally, analyzing theories on women's integration into development and exploring the origins and manifestations of women's subordination, oppression, sexism and patriarchy. They have also examined gender inequalities and their intersections with class, nationality and race, as well as barriers to education and employment. Additionally, conversations about sexuality have highlighted the importance of bodily autonomy and the control of fertility and sexuality. In the 1980s, African women contested feminist portrayals of FGM as "barbaric" practices suppressing sexuality. They questioned the lack of attention that the high rates of maternal mortality received. Today, awareness campaigns about sexuality are increasingly vital, supporting broader initiatives like family planning and HIV/AIDS prevention.

Lastly, research on masculinity as a construct in culture and tradition, conducted by both men and women, is of critical importance. This research challenges male researchers to understand and deconstruct patriarchal institutions rooted in African culture, politics and religion. Even nationalists who have resisted the authoritarianism and conservatism of both colonial and postcolonial regimes often fail to acknowledge the ideological foundations that perpetuate gender disparities. They show no concerns over the marginalization and exclusion of women from decision-making bodies and the violation of women's rights in constitutions, family laws, labor codes and religious codes. Advocacy for affirmative action and gender parity is often met with skepticism and ridicule. It is crucial to dismantle the mechanisms of male violence against women, whether in the home, the workplace, or a war zone, and to examine the forces that lead to appalling acts like the gang rape of girls by rebels or soldiers during conflicts.

Understanding Gender and Advancing Women's Causes for Greater Social Justice

Despite facing criticism as being Eurocentric, the concept of gender is increasingly making inroads within women's discourse. It serves as an analytical tool to better understand the power dynamics between men and women across various contexts, including the family, workplace and political sphere. This concept helps identify not only the prevalent forms of dominance, but also subtle and pervasive inequalities often justified by cultural, religious or political beliefs.

Through debates sparked during prominent international events,[16] discussions on women's issues have broadened and helped to frame their fundamental rights as universal human rights. This discourse on human rights has become a pivotal analytical and advocacy tool for African feminist and women's organizations. It has empowered them to more effectively address and articulate concerns relevant to them, leveraging both national and international networks. The slogan "women's rights are human rights," popularized during the 1993 Vienna conference, has gained widespread traction. This rallying cry has captured the attention of both the African populace and its political representatives, prompting responses ranging from moderate to more assertive activism.

Across the continent, governments have signed numerous international conventions, including the 1979 UN Convention on the Elimination of All Forms of Discrimination Against Women (CEDAW). Despite reservations about specific provisions – such as banning polygamy, ensuring abortion rights, and abolishing female genital mutilation – they have established institutions and adopted policies that Amina Mama described in 1996 as the "emergence of state feminism." After over a decade of advocacy by women, an additional protocol concerning women's rights was attached to the African Charter on Human and Peoples' Rights (1981), which included appointing a woman as the African Union's special rapporteur on women's rights. This protocol made significant legal advances, including the abolition of polygamy and female genital mutilation, and the right to abortion in cases of incest or rape. In the past 20 years, other instruments have been adopted to promote and ensure economic, social and cultural rights, providing a basis to demand appropriate measures for turning equality in theory into equality in practice. Additionally, African women managed to place the rights of girls on the agenda at the 1995 Beijing World Conference on Women, aligning with the proposals of the 1990 UN Convention on the Rights of the Child.

Integrating women's issues into discussions about the African state opens new lines of inquiry that are often overlooked in conventional research on state politics. In a context where most women are excluded from decision-making bodies and broader political concerns, state interventions have paradoxically enabled some progress, at least in certain countries. Despite their general tendency toward authoritarianism, or in the rare instances when they act as welfare states, many governments have initiated a range of actions aimed at women – some deliberate, others to achieve compliance or due to international pressure. These include policies and programs for "protection," such as enhancing maternal and child health services dating back to the colonial era, establishing family planning, improving girls' education, and promoting income-generating activities and access to credit. Often ahead of the societies they represent and sometimes contrary to them, states have passed laws more favorable to women, although the effectiveness of these laws remains questionable. For example, Burkina Faso, Senegal, Togo and Côte d'Ivoire have legally banned FGM, while Kenya narrowly failed to pass a similar law by one vote in December 1998. At the same time, Senegal enhanced its Penal Code on violence against women, turning domestic violence – previously considered less severe if occurring within the family – into a harshly penalized offense during a 1999 revision of the Penal Code.

The law plays a crucial role in either eliminating, maintaining or reinforcing discrimination against women. We cannot improve their status without the proper legal tools. In areas like sexuality and fertility, which influence women's family, social, economic and political status, as well as their relationships with men and their freedoms, the impact of laws on the ability of women to make their own decisions is profound. On the other hand, it is crucial to question the nature of laws that claim to serve the greater good in theory while being largely patriarchal in practice. Family codes exemplify this. In countries where they have been enacted after the abolition of previously existing colonial codes, their stated goal has been to "protect" women[17] rather than grant them rights that lead to true equality. While there are steps toward more equal relationships, deep-seated legal inequalities persist.

The role of women in politics is perhaps the most debated topic today. At the 1995 World Conference on Women in Beijing, governments recognized that "the empowerment of women and their full participation on an equal basis in all areas of social life, including decision-making and access to power, are essential for equality, development, and peace." Over the last decade, the uneven deployment of democracy in Africa has spurred discussions about freedoms and a reclamation of these freedoms by the public. Despite the low level of women's involvement in administrative, union and political decisions – a reflection of their marginalized status in both family and society – their position has evolved. Over the past two decades, it has shifted from merely voicing concerns within policy discussions to actively pushing for inclusion in decision-making processes.

These struggles against discrimination and sexism are part of broader movements that see women actively engaging in political and economic struggles across the continent. Feminists have not only challenged gender relations in the Global South but also tied these inequalities to a global economic order that perpetuates disparity. During 1980's World Conference on Women in Copenhagen, Western feminists attributed sexism as the source of their problems, while women from the Global South called attention to imperialism, the international division of labor, and unequal economic exchanges. Works such as *Femmes et multinationales* (Michel, Diarra and Dos Santos-Agbessy 1981) and *Patriarchy and Accumulation on a World Scale* (Mies 1986) aimed to contextualize gender and class inequalities within dominant patriarchal economic systems. Throughout Africa, the diminishing capacity of societies to provide decent living conditions has forced populations to adopt precarious survival strategies.

In an edited volume for DAWN,[18] *The Marketization of Governance: Feminist Perspectives from the Global South* (2000), Viviene Taylor gathers together articles from DAWN feminists across Africa, Asia, Latin America, Central America and the Pacific. These articles delve into pressing issues, many of which speak directly to Africa's political reshaping and social transformations. Over the past three decades, economic and political disasters such as debt burdens, structural adjustment policies, transitional democratic phases, financial liberalization and geopolitical conflicts have severely impacted women. Despite ongoing discussions about advancing women's rights, these rights have significantly deteriorated. State cutbacks and the privatization of essential public services like healthcare, education, water and electricity have shifted responsibilities away from governments and onto citizens, especially women, who frequently head households. Global economic integration has jeopardized achievements in securing citizenship and reproductive rights, as well as access to natural, material and financial resources. This situation poses a critical question: "How can we convert these theoretical advances and paper guarantees into real social change?" (Taylor 2000:2). This is precisely what gender analysis aims to accomplish – moving beyond just describing and analyzing gender-stratified social facts to transforming the socially constructed gender relations to achieve equality and social justice in Africa.

2.4 Conclusion

Advances in women's studies and the use of gender analysis to explore societal roles have transformed research across social, economic, religious and political spheres. It is important to recall that questions around gender stem from women's studies and are intrinsically connected to them. This approach has significantly refreshed African research, which has traditionally been male-dominated and often indifferent to the question of women. It has brought to light the dynamics of power between men and women, putting on vivid display their socially constructed and political nature. As a form of praxis, gender analysis helps expose and dismantle male dominance and various other forms of oppression. It lays the groundwork for critical questions about power dynamics within families, sexuality, fertility, health, links between economic and family relationships, management of natural resources, and political access, all within the context of the democratization of Africa.

The effort to reappropriate gender compels scholars across academia to critically examine and depart from traditional African sociopolitical, economic and cultural frameworks. This effort extends beyond simply including another chapter on women and gender in research – it demands a thorough re-evaluation of social phenomena as inherently gendered, affecting both women and men. The principal challenge is to shift the predominantly male perspectives and discourse in social research to better understand and facilitate the ongoing changes across Africa.

3

Feminist Movements in Africa (2012)[1]

During her studies at the University of Dakar in the early years of independence, Fatou Sow joined the Centre National de la Recherche Scientifique (CNRS), and successfully pursued a career as a sociologist, completing a thesis on Senegalese elites. Later, she qualified as a research director. Gradually, her academic interactions with colleagues from other countries led her to take an interest in sociological studies on women in African countries, and she became a committed feminist activist.

Alongside her research and teaching activities at Cheikh Anta Diop University in Dakar, she contributed in 1994 to the establishment of an annual Conference on Gender at the Council for the Development of Social Science Research in Africa (CODESRIA), aimed at training African scholars in gender-centric issues. She also co-edited the volume *Engendering African Social Sciences* (Imam et al. 1997). From 1998, she balanced a teaching career in Dakar with her research role at CNRS, at Paris Diderot University, in the laboratory Sociétés en développement dans l'espace et dans le temps (SEDET, or Societies in Development in Space and Time), founded by Catherine Coquery-Vidrovitch. In 1999, she organized in Dakar the second colloquium on francophone feminist research, whose proceedings were published under the title *La recherche féministe francophone. Langue, identités et enjeux* (Karthala, 2009). The partnerships she developed with American and

African universities around the 1990s enabled her to forge strong bonds between African feminists from both francophone and anglophone spheres. She has held prominent positions in several feminist networks, notably as the coordinator for Development Alternatives for Women in a New Era (DAWN) in Francophone Africa, a powerful network of feminists from the Global South whose research has been used for lobbying international institutions. A member and chair of the Reproductive Health Research Network in Francophone Africa (1994–6), she co-edited with Codou Bop *Notre corps, notre santé. Santé et sexualité des femmes en Afrique subsaharienne* (2004). Since 2008, she has been the coordinator of another research and advocacy network, Women Living Under Muslim Laws, based in Asia, Africa and the Middle East.

This interview focuses on the impact of feminist and women's movements across Africa, particularly in West Africa. While organized women's movements in Africa have grown stronger since the decolonial era, numerous women's associations and groups have roots that stretch back much further. These movements have seen significant growth since the 1990s and have increasingly solidified their institutional presence. They are comprised of women who are intellectuals, professionals, activists or members of local groups, all united by shared causes. These movements are now engaging in more politicized analyses of gender relations, patriarchal structures and the effects of colonial, postcolonial and current neoliberal policies on women, with a particular focus on women's living conditions and rights. However, they consciously distance themselves from Western feminist perspectives by adopting a "decolonial" approach, which sets out to dismantle Western conceptual frameworks. Building an African-centered feminist discourse remains a political challenge.

Christine Verschuur: We wanted to do this interview with you so that you could share with us your insights into the feminist and women's movements across African countries.

Since you brought up the term "feminist," let me state that it's a label I embrace willingly and even proudly. In Africa, people imagine all kinds of different things when they hear this word, but it certainly grabs their attention. For me, embracing this label allows me to move beyond conventional discussions about women and the "familiar territory" where many African women stake their claims while advocating for women's rights without really challenging the dominant patriarchal system. Patricia McFadden, a committed feminist from Swaziland, has called attention to this problem. It's also essential to distinguish between feminist movements and women's movements. Their relationship is extremely complex, as they find themselves at times aligning with key issues and working together to tackle them, and at others starkly divided and on opposite sides of significant debates. Feminist organizations often bring new issues concerning women into public debate while women's organizations, which generally have a more moderate tone and are therefore more readily received, are more likely to get these issues on the agendas of governments. Of course, the path from here is never straight, as we experience as many setbacks as we do triumphs.

Blandine Destremau: That wasn't our first question, but maybe it's a good place to start. Since you brought up the difference between these two terms, perhaps we could go deeper into the history of women's movements and feminist movements.

In an article I wrote on African women's appropriation of gender (Sow 2007 [chapter 2 above]), I explored the history of diverse movements that emerged from various regions as well as from different metaphysical, religious and political traditions. I will touch on this briefly to provide some background, but I remain mindful of the fact that the focus of our interview is on the experiences of Africans.

It's important to emphasize that Africa is a continent rich with varied historical and cultural experiences and diverse political, economic and social contexts. This diversity informs my approach. Women's histories, like those of any group of people, continue to reflect this diversity, despite the leveling effects of globalization. My comments concern the African continent, more specifically West Africa and Senegal where I have lived and conducted most of my research.

First, it's important to understand that the officially recognized women's movements we see today, with their own idioms, protocols and forms of organization, are relatively new developments. These movements date back to the colonial era from which they, along with many other local institutions, adopted their organizational models. However, this doesn't mean that women's organizations didn't exist before or that they failed to address issues pertinent to women. Even today, women continue to create novel support networks and group structures to work through problems they share based on their age, origins and social status. There is an abundance of literature on this subject, which I will only touch on briefly here to make my argument clear.

The decolonial era can serve as a relatively reasonable historical reference to explain the evolution of women's movements in contemporary Africa. The first movements to gain official recognition, giving them a platform and the ability to engage with people in powerful positions, were in fact enabled by those same people in powerful positions. Every new regime propped up a women's movement that was bound in many ways to the single or dominant party. Civil society organizations, a term that later entered the political vocabulary, didn't enjoy the same level of support (Monga 1995). They were even regularly accused of bolstering the opposition.

Other, more popular, women's organizations have not sought official recognition. With a more extended history and larger membership, these groups have developed extensive networks of women centered on kinship, community ties and a variety of exchanges that support both social and economic activities. *Mbootaay* (women's associations) serve as a fundamental resource in Wolof society, highlighting the significant role women play in managing social relations through various ceremonies that mark the obligatory stages of individual and collective life, from birth to death (Sow 1975). Tontines foster another form of solidarity, based on saving money.

These savings clubs maintain another form of solidarity based on the accumulation of savings. They have often been the only way for women to accumulate some capital by pooling and sharing resources – nowadays money – to meet needs, fulfill various family and social obligations, and fund economic activities (Mottin-Sylla 1987). The practice, still essential from an economic standpoint, continues today in the same way: the agreements underlying them are still based on verbal and moral commitments. However, the amounts involved, their allocation and their uses have evolved significantly, as shown by Moya's 2011 study of tontines in a suburban neighborhood of Dakar. This practice also extends into Senegalese and other African communities living abroad (Semin 2011). Amidst these diverse grassroots organizations and colonial-era political movements, a plethora of friendly societies, trade groups and professional associations has emerged, which have undoubtedly fueled broader social movements.

The explosion of the women's movement from the 1980s and 1990s can be attributed to several factors. The United Nations Decade for Women served as a catalyst, even amidst the many challenges and disillusionments. During this period, discourses and initiatives were often shaped by diverse agendas, leading to outcomes that varied widely – some were meaningful, while others proved to be illusory or trivial, as Jules Falquet (2003) eloquently explains. African women have come together locally as well as across the continent, recognizing the opportunity to unite and use their emerging political visibility to advance their agenda on a larger scale. This shift also reflects a change in how women are perceived, moving away from being mired in the burdens of their environment and the inability to benefit from development and progress, as if "the African man hasn't yet fully entered into history," to echo the statement made by President Nicolas Sarkozy at Cheikh Anta Diop University in Dakar in 2007.[2] Decades after gaining independence, they have entered the twenty-first century with specific demands: to give birth in maternity wards rather than at home, even though local midwives are better trained; to pursue gainful employment that extends beyond just rural and artisanal work; to engage more actively in political life, and so on. They have established a large number of organizations, economic associations, and appear increasingly determined to advance their interests in a radically new global context. They have played a significant role in the "World March of Women," initially a predominantly Western movement. Through bilateral, international and UN cooperation, they have effectively elevated women's issues on the global political agenda.

C.V.: All these women's movements you mention fought for various causes. Would you say they were motivated in particular by "feminist" issues? Was there an awareness of gender inequalities within these societies?

During the 1960s and 1970s, rural women's organizations were not "official" movements, but rather groupings of women based on social relations they had forged among themselves. In contrast, many urban associations began to position themselves in dialogue with the government (usually a single political party), establishing offices, electing a president and treasurer, and recruiting members. They occupied the political space without gaining decision-making power. It was impossible to discuss gender relations due to the "politically correct" discourse associated with the fight against imperialism. The colonial, and later neocolonial, order could be challenged, but it was more difficult to criticize the order established by the Founding Fathers of Independence.

I lived through this history and remember that the first Senegalese women's organizations were social clubs and professional associations for female teachers, midwives, lawyers and so on, in local branches of international organizations (*Soroptimist, Zonta*). All of them vehemently refused the label of "feminist." And yet they advocated for better living and health conditions, access to education, training and employment, advancement within the civil service – the best path to social mobility at the time – and representation in power structures.[3] However, at no point did they challenge the political and social patriarchal system or question the prevailing cultural norms. They only spoke out against a few practices they considered excessive, such as the costs of family ceremonies or dowry expectations. Any other attempt to challenge social norms was viewed as being influenced by foreign pressure. Adopting a critical stance was difficult in an era dominated by nationalist discourse focused on culture, Negritude and African identity, promoted by Senghor, the poet-president, and Cheikh Hamidou Kane, the gifted Senegalese author of *L'aventure ambiguë*. Questioning gender relations was seen as denying the complementary roles that women themselves still largely embraced. In my first article on women, published in 1963 in the inaugural issue of *Awa* magazine,[4] I defended the complementarity of these relations. The inequalities denounced by women were primarily those produced by the colonial – and, subsequently, neocolonial – order. *La civilisation de la femme dans la tradition africaine* (SAC 1974) set the tone for the debates of the time. The first African feminists would go on to adopt a discourse on unequal exchange and discuss its impact on women during debates surrounding the dependency and development theories of the 1970s and 1980s. *Femmes et multinationales* (1981), edited by Andrée Michel, Agnès-Fatoumata Diarra and Hélène Dos Santos-Agbessy, which gathered together the proceedings of a conference of the same name, is a perfect embodiment of the debates of the time.

Women have always faced significant challenges, in both the past and the present. But the extent to which these issues are feminist remains unclear. It all depends on one's interpretation of feminism. This is an ongoing debate that feminists across the world are engaged in. Who has the authority, the power or the legitimacy to define what feminism is? While some women fight to improve their conditions, they distance themselves from a version of feminism that others fervently embrace.

Gender inequality, a core issue for feminists, has been a major point of contention in discussions among both African and Western women, as well as within African communities themselves. This issue was primarily raised by female intellectuals. Moreover, the fight for equality wasn't quick to take hold amid the competing demands of development. It was largely viewed as a concern of feminists from the Global North, whereas African women prioritized improving their own living standards. Particularly since the onset of the UN Decade for Women, there has been a pressing need to "decolonize" thought and research. This imperative was highlighted by the Association of African Women for Research and Development at its inception in 1977. It's important to note that the debate was predominantly conducted in English, with francophone scholars having little exposure to American scholarship in this area. This field was, above all, a domain of expertise for English speakers. Women's studies began to be institutionalized in the United States, while this was not yet part of the curriculum in African universities.

B.D.: With feminists from the Global North? Or from everywhere?

During major international conferences on women and other pressing issues of those times, African women expressed concerns about feminist positions that didn't always align with their priorities or made them feel marginalized. These concerns emerged out of a context in which African men and women were actively working to decolonize every field of knowledge (economics, politics, history and so on). This effort is still under way. In 2007, CODESRIA introduced an initiative to spark further research on Africa titled: "Decolonizing the Social Sciences in Africa: A Map Forward." For scholars and activists, there was hesitancy to engage with the dominant feminist discourse, which was framed in Western terms. There were many valid reasons for this. The need for a definitive break was perceived as an essential and *politically correct* step. It's worth recalling that African participants at the Conference on Women in National Development, held at Wellesley College (1976), were "outraged" by what they viewed as the arrogance of American feminist scholars (Mernissi 1984). Many of them, like Fatima Mernissi and Filomena Chioma Steady, both sociology professors in Morocco and Sierra Leone respectively, or Achola Pala of Kenya, who became a UNIFEM (United Nations Development Fund for Women) official, built their illustrious careers by focusing on women's issues. They pushed for the creation of the Association of African Women for Research and Development (AAWORD), which advocated for a feminism rooted in decolonized sources, influences and ideas. The demand was such that in its early years, AAWORD refused membership to non-African feminists, even if they lived in Africa and worked on issues specific to African women. F. Steady and A. Pala collaborated extensively to develop a theoretical framework for addressing women's issues in Africa. Similarly, feminist movements in Latin America and Asia, including the feminists' network of the Global South, DAWN – of which I was a member from 1994 to 2006 – also sought to break away from the prevailing feminist ideology.

C.V.: Were there other schools of thought among these groups of "feminist" women? Do you feel their perspectives mainly overlapped, or were there noticeable tensions – perhaps between the more urban elite women, who were highly educated, and other women?

For me, your question raises a concern about the women you refer to as the urban, highly educated elite. There's a tendency to think of them as being out of touch with other women in their country or region, despite their involvement in both national and global movements. I share Amina Mama's view of this, which she expressed in the editorial of the inaugural issue of *Feminist Africa*: "In African contexts, feminism has emerged out of women's deep engagement with and commitment to national liberation, so it is hardly surprising that African women's movements today feature in the disparate struggles and social movements characterizing post-colonial life. African women are mobilizing at local, regional and international levels, and deploying various strategies and forms" (2002:1).

This is the same way Peggy Antrobus frames the global women's movement in her examination of its history and evolution: "The role of the activist/scholar, grounded in feminist theory, was crucial in this process of transforming the work of traditional women's organizations and bureaucratic initiatives into part of a political movement" (2004:47). These feminists belong to groups that vary from purely intellectual circles to organizations, or both, where they engage in discussions about feminist theories, issues, and their relevance to the situation of African women. AAWORD (1977) was the first attempt on a continental scale to stake out a space distinct from the dominant feminist discourses. The organization brought together women from diverse geographic, professional and ideological backgrounds to establish African perspectives. Following this initiative, other organizations were formed, some influenced by this experience and others driven by entirely different concerns. Several African publications have offered a thorough critique of gender studies (Steady 1981; Mama 1996; Imam, Mama and Sow 1997; Lewis 2002; Oyéwùmí 1997; Osha 2006, etc.).

To give a simplified overview of a very complex field, allow me to cite two journals that represent radically opposed approaches to feminism in Africa: *Jenda, A Journal of Culture and African Women Studies*, and *Feminist Africa*, both established in 2001 (both are available online). Although they address similar socio-cultural, political and economic concerns of women, their methodologies differ significantly. *Jenda* dismisses feminist and gender-centric approaches, which it considers Western, advocating instead for a distinctly African perspective on the question of women. Conversely, *Feminist Africa* adopts these concepts, analyzing and situating them within a critical examination of their impact on African societies. African feminist theories and analyses typically fluctuate between these contrasting positions.

From the very first issue of *Jenda*, the editor Nkiru Nzegwu established its viewpoint in the editorial:

> In our view, one of the major ill effects of globalization and the universal deployment of Americentrism is the marginalization of peoples, cultures, paradigms, values and ideas that are in opposition to this dominant creed. Given that multiplicity of paradigms is crucial to theoretical study, it is important to provide critical space to ideas that have not been accorded visibility in the global arena due to lack of representation. (2001:13)

This issue stands as a rejection of a Western perspective on women, in the spirit of several seminal works such as *Male Daughters, Female Husbands: Gender and Sex in an African Society* (1987) and *Re-Inventing Africa: Matriarchy, Religion, and Culture* (1998) by Amadiume, or *The Invention of Women: Making an African Sense of Western Gender Discourses* by Oyéwùmí (1997). A clear line of continuity can be drawn between these works, which are equally aligned with *La civilisation de la femme dans la tradition africaine* (SAC 1974) or *L'union matrimoniale dans la tradition des peuples noirs* (Camara and Kanji 2000). The core argument is that African women have traditionally held significant power within the family and community, across both religious and political spheres. This stands in contrast to the marginal roles of women described by Western feminists. These feminists critique gender relations that are oppressive to women, arguing that these relations are based on a "universal" inequality between men and women. In the second volume of *Jenda*, dedicated to "Feminism in Africa," Oyèrónké Oyéwùmí, another towering figure, dismisses the concepts of gender and womanhood, the binary distinction between men and women, and the notion of inherent gender inequality, explaining that:

> The difficulty of applying feminist concepts to express and analyze African realities is the central challenge of African gender studies. The fact that Western gender categories are presented as inherent in nature (of bodies) and operate on a dichotomous, binarily opposed male/female, man/woman duality in which the male is assumed to be superior and therefore the defining category, is particularly alien to many African cultures. When African realities are interpreted based on these Western claims, what we find are distortions, obfuscations in language and often a total lack of comprehension due to the incommensurability of social categories and institutions. (2002:6–7)

A journal from the University of Cape Town, available online and in print, *Feminist Africa* takes a contrary stance. It confirms its feminist mission right there in the title of the journal. Amina Mama, the journal's editor and director of the African Gender Institute at the University of Cape Town, outlines its purpose and goals: "The decision to embark on the strategy of producing an overtly feminist scholarly journal grounded in African contexts [...] is part of our ongoing suite of activities, all of which address the challenge of producing people seriously equipped to contribute to democratic transformation in a region where feminism clearly has a pivotal role to play" (2001:2).

Without denying the influence of African cultures on women's roles, she advances this editorial line because, she claims:

> Feminism – an international political and intellectual movement to challenge the subordination of women – has many roots and trajectories. The theoretical and practical aspects of this movement draw connections between the local and the global manifestations of women's ongoing subordination, across the various movements that seek to advance liberation and development, and across the various academic disciplines that organize social theory. (2004:121)

I share this view and this approach, which mixes rigorous research with personal reflection by drawing on all the theoretical tools best suited to these purposes. We can go into this in more detail later if you like.

B.D.: Would you say that what you have described in terms of the distrust toward the risk of Westernization, the risk of being accused of Westernization, is evolving today into a genuine form of thinking that positions itself at a distance, and could we possibly describe this form of thinking as postcolonial? Do you identify with this term, and do you believe that this history has led to a reflection that is both feminist and postcolonial?

The distrust is certainly softening, though its effects can still be seen in women's organizations, academia and public opinion. It's well known that universities are hesitant to establish women's studies centers. Anglophone universities are notably ahead of their francophone counterparts in this respect. Anytime the promotion of women seems to challenge African cultural norms, it's deemed dangerous and understood to be influenced by foreign intervention.

It's worth asking: Whose universalism are we talking about? Whose interpretations and concerns among Africans are being addressed? These questions warrant a more thorough analysis. I often go back to Bakare-Yusuf's response to what Oyéwùmí calls the "invention of women" by the West, and the rejection of Western theories, which is, in fact, more often than not a rejection of the theories tied to women's studies:

> Most importantly, we must reject outright any attempt to assign a particular conceptual category as belonging only to the "West" and therefore inapplicable to the African situation. For millennia, Africa has been part of Europe as Europe has been part of Africa, and out of this relation, a whole series of borrowed traditions from both sides have been and continue to be brewed and fermented. To deny this intercultural exchange and reject all theoretical imports from Europe is to violate the order of knowledge and simultaneously disregard the contribution of various Africans to European cultural and intellectual history and vice versa. Finally, asserting a polytheistic approach to understanding Yoruba (and other African) social dynamics does not lead to an outright rejection of Oyewumi's theorization of seniority. Rather, what is now required is to open up a space where a multiplicity of contradictory existences and conceptual categories can be productively engaged within our theorizing. It is this way that we can understand and maintain Africa and local knowledge in the plural. (Bakare-Yusuf 2002:11)

For more than three decades, we've been working to decolonize research. As a result, we often find ourselves caught up in deconstructing Western feminist discourse rather than creating our own by drawing on a diverse array of sources. Their discourse on themselves and on us should really be their problem, not ours. As Abena Busia, a Ghanaian scholar, notes perceptively, "One of the more tortured aspects of feminist praxis in the West is the difficulty many Euro-American women confront in yielding the assumed authority of their theoretical paradigms in the face of other systems of thought, and other modes of practice and negotiation as presented by Women of Color about our own lived experiences" (1994: iv).

I would prefer to set aside that concern and focus on the goals of the African Feminist Forum, established in 2006, which states in its charter's preamble: "We claim the right and the space to be African feminists" (2006:7) – and to fight against the subordination of women. It's still problematic to deny the sexism inherent in our cultures, the differences in status, and the inequalities between men and women, which are exacerbated by ongoing political, economic, cultural and religious changes. Indeed, factors like age or class play a role, but they shouldn't overshadow the significant impact of gender. As Amina Mama has pointed out (2003), serious critiques have been leveled at the positions represented by "Women in Development" and "Gender and Development," even by African women themselves.[5] Gender theory as articulated by any number of prominent figures, from Joan Scott to Judith Butler, from Simone de Beauvoir to Christine Delphy, Nicole-Claude Mathieu or Elisabeth Badinter, has been subject to critical scrutiny, especially in academic contexts. We have long grappled with translating and appropriating gender concepts and social relations between men and women. But should we entirely dismiss feminist critique simply because it doesn't conform to African cultural norms?

We could debate endlessly the concepts of matriarchy and patriarchy and their impact on African women.[6] More pertinent to this discussion in my mind is the concept of matrilineality (rather than matriarchy), which assigns different societal roles to men and women and shapes the power dynamics between them. This is clear in social and familial systems where matrilineality was predominant, including the transfer of power and property through the maternal line and the significant role of maternal uncles in raising nephews. However, even within these systems, men typically held dominant positions, often with the uncle or brother serving as the head of the family. Islam, Christianity and colonial laws have profoundly altered these systems. Nowadays, matrilineal and patrilineal systems either coexist or are interwoven, depending on the context. Without delving into kinship ties here, it's worth noting that the aunts on both the father's and mother's sides play varying roles, sometimes symbolic and sometimes real, within the family (Diop 1985). Patriarchy, which comes in many forms, deeply structures contemporary societies and significantly influences the lives of women.

Seniority, a concept central to Oyèrónké Oyéwùmí's thinking (1997), is a clear factor in social stratification (elder versus younger), which has been extensively documented by French anthropologists who have highlighted its role in systems of production. However, for women, recognition of seniority comes much later in life, often not until menopause, when they finally gain authority.

Motherhood is currently being re-examined and redefined through new theoretical frameworks. This was a key focus at the "Images of Motherhood, African and Nordic Perspectives" symposium, held in Gorée, Senegal, in 2003. Signe Arnfred from the Nordic Africa Institute, one of the event's organizers, pushed to redefine its core meaning. She called attention to the stark contrast between women of the Global North, who often downplay the role of motherhood, and African womanists, who emphasize the revered status of mothers in their cultures. Renowned African American sociologist Niara Sudarkasa, author of *The Strength of Our Mothers: African and African American Women and Families – Essays and Speeches* (1997), stressed the pivotal role of mothers in African American families, a significance rooted in the historical context of slavery. In a special online issue of *Jenda* dedicated to the symposium's proceedings, Oyèrónké Oyéwùmí, who didn't attend the symposium, contributed an article that also celebrated motherhood: "Motherhood occupies a special place in African cultures and societies. Regardless of whether a particular African society displays a patrilineal or matrilineal kinship system, mothers are the essential building block of social relationships, identities, and indeed society. Because mothers symbolize familial ties, unconditional love, and loyalty, motherhood is invoked even in extrafamilial situations that call upon these values" (2003:1).

As a participant in the symposium, I pointed out that mothers hold a significant place tied to their reproductive roles in African cultures, as in other human cultures. The veneration of the Virgin Mary is a symbol of this. I also acknowledged the role of women in managing social relationships. Without revisiting the critical analyses of motherhood, I emphasized the impact of "forced reproduction" (Mathieu 1985) on women's health, which is a major factor driving the alarmingly high rates of maternal mortality. Have women ever possessed the power to decide how many children they'd like to have, or even whether they'd like to have children at all? When will they really be able to claim that the decision of when or whether to have children is their choice to make? The experience of motherhood, as

Patricia McFadden points out, can "easily become a trap." Thus, "we need to understand the limits of our nurturing" (1997:1). Control over fertility, and thus sexuality, is a fundamental right that, still today, requires our active defense.

C.V.: What can we say about grassroots women's organizations, economic interest groups and farmer cooperatives that might not explicitly identify with feminism, yet are actively involved in shifting the power dynamics between men and women through their actions? What is the relationship between these organizations, which are rapidly transforming gender power relations, and urban feminist intellectuals who champion a feminist discourse? In Latin America, discussions often focus on popular feminisms versus institutionalized feminisms in academia, government feminisms and the NGO-ization of the movement, among other distinctions and divisions. Is this also the case in Africa?

In her 1996 work *Études par les femmes et études sur les femmes en Afrique durant les années 1990* (*Women's Studies and Studies on Women during the 1990s*), Amina Mama provides an excellent analysis of the various forms of organizations related to women's issues: women's organizations, feminist organizations, state feminists or "femocrats." These same distinctions are found in the rest of the world, including in Europe and North America. Women's movements have existed in pre-colonial, colonial, and postcolonial Africa. Women have formed social networks and mobilized around a range of issues, as documented by the series Women Writing Africa – Les femmes écrivent l'Afrique. Esi Sutherland-Addy and Aminata Diaw illustrate this in their 2007 work *Des femmes écrivent l'Afrique: l'Afrique de l'Ouest et le Sahel* (*Women Writing Africa: West Africa and the Sahel*).

There is a wide range of relationships and viewpoints between grassroots organizations and elite women, from the most conservative women's groups to the more radical ones. In some cases, their views are irreconcilable. In others, despite conflicting motivations and approaches, discussions can lead to agreements. Feminists often help raise awareness about various issues and, at the same time, are reminded through these frequent interactions when their goals are too lofty. These interactions involve as much confrontation as they do negotiation over perspectives, languages and action strategies, aiming to reach a consensus when possible. Intellectuals, not always at the forefront of progressive ideas, are often forced to make compromises. For example, we've managed to generate discussions on women's reproductive rights without necessarily addressing their right to sexual pleasure. Each of us bears some responsibility in advancing women's rights. Today, grassroots organizations are taking up feminist positions, not only regarding contraception but also regarding access to land, credit, education and political decision-making. At the World Social Forum in Dakar (2011), many banners testified to a growing awareness of women's right to escape poverty.

The "NGO-ization" of women's movements dates back to the 1980s–1990s when international cooperation initiatives, inspired by the UN Decade for Women, began launching targeted projects. This period also saw governments cutting social spending due to structural adjustment policies. NGOs, funded by these international partnerships, stepped in to fill the void left by governments. Women's empowerment initiatives accelerated the NGO-ization of women's organizations. Governments worldwide established women's groups using a standardized organizational model with formal offices, and promoted income-generating projects.

B.D.: Would you say that the various movements have found ways of working together?

Despite class barriers, I do believe an alliance is being formed to take on shared struggles. Issues such as family code reforms, condemning violence against women, abolishing female genital mutilation (FGM) and early marriages, and the pressures to have children resonate at various levels across society. Issues like unequal inheritance rights, repudiation or the privileging of masculinity affect all Muslim families.

Many issues shocked public opinion when they were first brought up. In Senegal, discussions initiated by Awa Thiam in 1967 about FGM, as well as debates on violence against women led by the feminists of *Yewwu Yewwi*, caused an uproar among both men and women. Today, these same issues have essentially become common topics of conversation at the kitchen table.

C.V.: And what are your thoughts on "gender expertise"?

It has advanced the careers of many women and ... men! All the better for employment. Hiring boomed just to staff the growing number of these programs that sought to integrate women into development. It helped to broaden perspectives around women's issues. Unfortunately, the transition from Women in Development (WID) to Gender and Development (GAD) occurred without gender experts attending to the political dimension of these concepts as the United Nations and national governments had intended. As a result, the concept of gender, which is primarily about power dynamics, has been largely stripped of its critical charge. It was easily co-opted while its feminist dimension was dismissed as being too radical. This co-optation is the real danger.

C. V.: Do you think these gender experts, who are in turn training others to be experts in gender, can really be feminist?

It's possible, but it's complicated. For many of these experts, this is primarily a career opportunity rather than an ideological debate. It's difficult to openly engage in feminist debates, regardless of one's position on the issues. Identifying as a feminist or advocating for feminist ideals can be challenging in societies where there is significant resistance to social change. There is a growing awareness regarding a range of feminist issues, but little action to change the existing social order out of fear of being labeled a pawn of Western ideology. Therein lies the danger, as many positions on these issues are misrepresented or distorted. While women's issues are frequently acknowledged, they remain peripheral in decision-making processes. They are often evoked in policy proposals but rarely implemented. Essentially, it's merely paying lip service to women.

Ideas often fester in people's minds for a long time. Then, suddenly, something shifts, and once-taboo topics are openly discussed. FGM, for example, was initially banned more for medical reasons than due to concerns about sexual rights. During the 1980s and 1990s, sexuality could only be discussed in heterosexual terms. Debates over sexuality, initially expressed through music and other cultural forms, later spilled into mainstream media, leading to a more widespread denunciation of sexual abuse. There is an increasing number of conversations about homosexuality and decriminalization, but there's still a lot of pushback when we talk about sexual orientation as a right. Making progress on these issues won't be easy, but at least we can start to see a way forward.

C.V.: Just one last question: Are there any key figures who hold symbolic or historical importance for feminists? I'm reminded of a midwife from Mali who published her memoirs.

You're referring to *Femme d'Afrique* by Aoua Kéita (1975) who, in my opinion, was primarily a symbol of the anti-colonial struggle in French Sudan, like many of those who came before us and who set a precedent we aim to follow. Figures like Aoua Kéita or Alin Sitoë Diatta from Senegal are more icons of resistance against colonial rule than symbols of feminism. They demonstrated that women could challenge the colonial order through political action. In this regard, they are our "heroines." But they never challenged the patriarchal order.

C.V.: What do you personally think about the concept of gender?

Although it isn't uncommon for African women to use the term "gender," I am increasingly reluctant to use it myself, especially in public discussions. These days, I prefer to talk about the feminist perspective. Gender was once a valuable concept for thinking about power dynamics, but today, the concept of gender, as the United Nations has reinterpreted it, has lost its force and pertinence in Africa. Governments favor it over any feminist rhetoric. For the majority of men, "gender relations" implies no conflict; it simply refers to relations between men and women. For them, these relationships are not based on inequality. The internationalization of the concept has robbed it of its disruptive potential. I often refer to the "social relations between sexes." We still have a tremendous amount of work to do. How do we convey the unequal power relations between men and women in our African languages?

PART TWO
HUMAN RIGHTS OF AFRICAN WOMEN
CONFRONTING RELIGIOUS AND POLITICAL FUNDAMENTALISM

4

Female Genital Mutilation and Human Rights in Africa (1998)[1]

4.1 Introduction

The gunfire had barely died down after several years of fratricidal conflict when Sierra Leone was back in the headlines in Africa again, this time for a different reason. The Senegalese daily *Le Soleil* reported a dispatch from the Agence France-Presse which stated: "Genital mutilation halted during Ramadan" (January 20, 1977). A few weeks earlier, the same news agency had reported an incident in a refugee camp in Grafton, about 100 kilometers from Freetown, the capital. During a mass ceremony, nearly 600 young girls were subjected to genital mutilation. This event might have gone unnoticed amid the usual flurry of African news if Doctors without Borders hadn't disclosed that around 100 victims needed emergency hospital care. The report also revealed that there was a Sierra Leonean association of circumcisers, influential enough to operate openly. In response to a media backlash fueled by activists, the association organized its own march in Freetown in support of its practice. Amid the outrage, the government chose to remain silent while the secretary of state for women's affairs decided to stay out of the affair.

In early 1996, the plight of a young Togolese woman captured international attention. She was imprisoned in the United States for illegal immigration under humiliating conditions. Yet she ultimately secured asylum with the help of women's organizations and human rights groups from the US and abroad. She claimed she was escaping the threat of genital mutilation in her village. Shortly before this case, a similar plea was made by an undocumented Guinean mother living in France. Facing deportation threats against her and her two children, her lawyers successfully argued that the girls were at risk of genital mutilation, leading to the French authorities granting her resident status.

This issue periodically resurfaces. Beyond the uproar at major conferences, it is the accidents from genital mutilations and their subsequent legal proceedings that bring the issue back into discussion. The first legal cases were pursued in France (Verdier 1990) in the early 1980s, when West African families were prosecuted following serious complications, including hemorrhages and deaths, in girls who had been subjected to genital mutilation on French soil. Local authorities were at a loss regarding how to deal with these unusual cases, struggling to invoke charges and issue sentences that were either seen as trivial, given the severe consequences of the mutilation, or too harsh for families who, adhering to their cultural norms, had not intended to cause the death of their children.[2] Over time, they began to issue stricter sentences, including prison terms. Other Western countries with sizable African immigrant populations, such as the UK, the Netherlands, Belgium, Finland, Italy and Canada, have also grappled with similar situations, each adopting different policies.[3] For instance, Italy, due to significant communities from countries like Somalia, Ethiopia, Sudan and Senegal, allowed the practice in hospitals to reduce medical risks (Smith 1995:158), making it perhaps the only Western country to officially condone the practice. However, most countries have done little to address the issue as it affects them minimally. Some have condemned female genital mutilation (FGM) on ethical grounds and, lacking specific legislation, have applied relevant penalties from their criminal codes, including France, the Netherlands, Denmark, Finland, Germany, Spain, Portugal, Switzerland and Australia. Sweden was the first in Europe to enact specific legislation against FGM in 1983,[4] followed by the UK in 1985,[5] Belgium in 1990, and Canada in 1992.[6] In the United States, after decades of advocacy since the 1970s, the government funded various initiatives aimed at eliminating the practice with the hope that eradication efforts would be led principally by the countries concerned. The Federal Prohibition of Female Genital Mutilation Act, passed on

September 30, 1996, and effective from March 29, 1997, represents a significant legislative advance.

Despite the numerous incidents of FGM in Africa, which lead to medical, psychological and even fatal complications, I cannot recall a single case that has been prosecuted or publicly condemned, even on moral grounds. "It was destiny!" is a phrase often heard in response to these complications.

What is the current situation regarding sexual mutilation in Africa today, after 20 years of controversy? How can we broaden public discussions in regions where the practice persists, move these debates forward, and take concrete steps toward abolishment? It is crucial to connect the conversation about FGM with the broader issue of women's rights, evaluate the progress and challenges, and leverage both national and international policies and legal frameworks to take on these deep-rooted customs. Ultimately, this is not just about ending harmful practices; it is about advancing women's rights.

4.2 Female Genital Mutilation: Where Are We Now?

It is estimated that about 115 million women worldwide have been subjected to genital mutilation (Hosken 1993). Most of them live in Africa. Indeed, in many African states, from Senegal to Nigeria, from Guinea to Somalia, including Mauritania, Chad, Northern Togo, Eritrea and Tanzania, FGM continues to be practiced, in the secluded areas of sacred groves and the courtyards of urban and suburban neighborhoods, in the name of cultural and religious traditions.

This practice impacts all ages, but it typically targets young girls, and increasingly infants, under the pretext that they are less sensitive to pain. In Mali, excision takes place between the 8th and 40th day after birth, a practice similar to that in northern and southwestern Nigeria. In Casamance, Senegal, it occurs between ages 3 and 6; in Burkina Faso, between 5 and 9; in Côte d'Ivoire, between 4 and 10; and elsewhere, during adolescence. Children of African immigrants, born and raised in France, Germany, Italy or the United States, are either subjected to excision locally or taken back to their home country during school holidays for the procedure, with or without parental consent. There are millions of cases where excision is carried out against the will of one or both parents, by the other spouse, the grandmother, the paternal aunt or another moral authority of the family or community. In Dakar, a Christian Sereer woman saw her two daughters literally abducted and excised by their paternal aunt of Mandeng origin. Neither she nor the girls had been prepared for the event. The paternal family's argument, presented much later, was the need for their "identity marking." Another Wolof woman had sworn on the Quran that her daughter, whose father is Hal Pulaar, would never be excised. A Malian gynecologist recounts in shocking detail how a patient she had successfully treated for years for infertility tragically lost her only child. The child, around the age of two, died from hemorrhaging after being excised without her mother's knowledge.

Genital mutilation can also be performed on adults, often due to intense social pressure. Women who escaped the practice at a younger age or come from different cultural backgrounds may agree to undergo excision before their marriage, sometimes on their wedding night, as observed in the Senegal River Valley (Mali, Mauritania, Senegal). The pressure to conform is significant. At a workshop on FGM in 1997, a participant from Burkina Faso recounted how a bankrupt man forced his wife to undergo excision, blaming her "impurity" for his financial ruin.[7] She was given a stark choice: excision or divorce. In Atakora, Togo, another participant reported that pregnant women are excised just before delivery, often when labor begins. In Togo, as well as in Mali, Senegal and other parts of Africa, unexcised girls are not permitted to serve meals due to perceived impurity. Among co-wives, those who are not excised face ostracism from those who are, and they may eventually give in to the practice. An extreme case is that of unexcised women in some Mauritanian communities, who cannot receive customary funeral rites. The family then performs the removal of the clitoris during the mortuary preparations.

At the same Rainbo–CIAF workshop on FGM in 1997, the various presentations on Burkina Faso, the host country, unanimously confirmed its high prevalence among all ethnic groups, both in Ouagadougou, the capital, and in rural areas (80 to 95%), regardless of religion (local religions in which everyone participates to varying degrees, Islam and Christianity). However, a significant reduction in the practice was noted among Protestant communities (70%), likely due to the efforts of their churches, while the rate remained high among immigrants from the surrounding region (87%).

Thus, there is a significant disparity between the decisions made at the international level by the United Nations to address women's struggles, and the ways in which these decisions are framed and implemented in the countries most affected. Actions that were initially modest evolved into progressively more forceful campaigns aimed at abolishing harmful practices. These efforts have taken place at local, national and international levels. In Africa, organizations began to form in the late 1970s, with varying levels of awareness, advocacy and action. To combat what they termed a "harmful" practice, they linked FGM with other harmful practices affecting mothers and children, such as early marriage and pregnancy, traditional childbirth methods and the force-feeding of young girls. It is believed that by addressing these broader health issues, they also made it easier to discuss the delicate subject of sexual mutilation at that time.

Initially, health-related arguments were pivotal in challenging the practice of FGM. When direct condemnation was not feasible, many organizations launched awareness campaigns. These campaigns informed women's groups, authorities and opinion leaders about the varied health risks associated with FGM, such as hemorrhages, urinary retention, infections (including genito-urinary infections, septicemia, adenitis, abscesses and tetanus), vesico-vaginal fistulas, premature labor, increased fetal–maternal morbidity and mortality, cysts, keloids, as well as various sexual health complications and mental health impacts.

Despite efforts to raise awareness of these somatic and psychological risks, the practice remains widespread. In some instances, medicalizing the procedure was proposed as a solution. For instance, in Egypt, shortly after the famous Cairo Conference (1994), under the pressure of religious groups, the medicalization of FGM was debated once again. It was suggested that cultural norms could continue to be respected as long as basic hygiene precautions, similar to those used in male circumcision, were taken. However, there has been substantial resistance to the issue of FGM since the 1930s. Local organizations reached a significant legal milestone in 1958 when President Nasser issued a decree condemning the practice, with penalties including imprisonment and fines. In 1959, a ruling from the Health

Ministry allowed for partial clitoridectomy, but only under conditions of consent from the woman and if the procedure was performed in a hospital.

It is clear that while debates on FGM are increasingly common in Africa and are being led by African women, these discussions are still hindered by taboos, modesty, revulsion and even annoyance. Various arguments, especially medical ones, are presented to the public to advocate for the abolition of FGM. But legal decisions that would strengthen the efforts of diverse activist groups are slow to materialize. After over 25 years of debate, the urgency to eliminate the practice has never been greater. We must demand the abolition of sexual mutilation and its criminalization, as a fundamental human right for women and girls, and fight for their right to physical and moral integrity.

4.3 FGM as a Women's Rights Issue and the Question of Terminology

The question of whether we should call this practice "female circumcision" or "female genital mutilation" has been a subject of lengthy debate. Currently, even among those who reject the practice, there is widespread resistance against calling excision "mutilation" since it is viewed as a cultural or social norm. To be sure, though, the terms used vary among authors or speakers, depending on whether their intent is to simply document the practice or to actively denounce it.

The term "mutilation" still shocks many, particularly among the communities involved, who view it as an affront to their cultural values. However, the resulting controversy has helped propel the discussion forward. At the 1980 World Conference on Women in Copenhagen, a heated debate erupted between African and Western women over how to label the practice: as circumcision or mutilation? African women criticized the Western feminist perspective as racist. Subsequent legal cases against immigrant families in France further heightened tensions. It wasn't until the Nairobi Conference that a meaningful dialogue began, where points of convergence and divergence were established among the diverse arguments related to culture, religion and women's rights.

Much has been said about customs or traditional practices. This was a key topic at a seminar held in Dakar in 1984, which focused on traditional practices affecting maternal and child health. The event led to the formation of the first pan-African organization on these issues, the Inter-African Committee.[8] Meanwhile, from the 1970s, some organizations have consistently labeled these practices as FGM. A notable example is the Commission pour l'abolition des mutilations sexuelles (CAMS) – or the Commission for the Abolition of Sexual Mutilation – deserving of special mention. This was founded by the Senegalese author Awa Thiam, known for her book *La parole aux négresses* (1978), during a time when there was little support for such outright denunciations in Africa. Indeed, at 1980's World Conference on Women in Copenhagen, many African organizations actively prevented her from speaking. Today, however, condemnation of these practices has grown, with support from international bodies such as the Research, Action, and Information Network for Bodily Integrity of Women (Rainbo),[9] along with various local and regional African organizations that advocate for women's rights.[10]

Today, African activists are increasingly denouncing female circumcision on the grounds of bodily autonomy. They also see it as an inherent form of violence. As Dr. Henriette Kouyaté clearly states, "any restructuring, shaping, or removal of any part of the genital organs is a mutilation and presents severe risk to the individual's health" (1990:3). But African public opinion, among both the general populace and the elite, continues to take offense when female circumcision is called mutilation, seeing no real difference between the rituals of male and female circumcision. To state the obvious, there are profound and unequivocal differences in both the nature and implications of male and female circumcision.

Male circumcision involves removing the foreskin, a procedure that generally doesn't cause medical complications unless performed under poor surgical or hygiene conditions. Traditionally, circumcision serves as a rite of passage from adolescence to adulthood and has been adopted or imposed by Islam within Muslim communities. Accompanying the procedure is an initiation into the community's values of wisdom, morality and religion. This ritual, which establishes a blood pact, strengthens group identity and fosters a sense of honor and brotherhood among those circumcised (*bokk lël*[11]). However, its intensity and significance have diminished over time. Nowadays, circumcision is typically performed at a younger age, between 5 and 8 years, and sometimes even on infants. The associated religious and educational values have evolved, replacing the concept of "brothers of *lël*" with that of school or university friends. In Senegal, regions like Casamance and the Bassari country still preserve some of the rite's initiatory values.[12] However, this is no longer the case in regions predominantly inhabited by groups such as the Pulaar, Wolof or Mandeng, which have a longer history of Islam, or in urban areas where the procedure is completely medicalized. It is projected that by 2015, 60 percent of Africans will live in urban areas. Muslim culture primarily maintains circumcision as a symbol of purification, essential not only for religious rites like prayer but also for daily cleanliness, which follows a specific ritual. While it is believed that circumcision enhances the sensitivity of the phallus, this belief underscores a broad valorization of the male genital organ and male sexual pleasure, viewing it as dominant and pleasure-giving. This raises important questions about the recognition of female sexuality and the conceptualization of women's bodies not merely as objects but as sexual subjects.

What is still referred to as female circumcision is quite different. It includes three types of procedures. Type I, clitoridectomy, involves the partial or total removal of the clitoris. Type II, excision, is the removal of both the clitoris and the labia minora. These first two types are the most prevalent, affecting 85 percent of women subjected to genital mutilation. Type III, infibulation, involves the removal of the clitoris and labia minora and the suturing of the labia majora, leaving only a small opening for the passage of urine and menstrual blood. This procedure, aimed at creating a smooth genital appearance (thus perceived as clean and beautiful), prevents any vaginal contact or sexual penetration. The genital area must be reopened for intercourse, typically on the wedding night. This practice affects 15 percent of mutilated women in regions like Northeast Africa – specifically Egypt, Mali and Northern Nigeria. More alarmingly still, in places such as Sudan, Somalia, Djibouti and Eritrea, between 80 and 90 percent of women experience this form of mutilation (Toubia 1995).

The effects of FGM on women's bodies also vary. Injuries to the female genital organs, ranging from mild to severe, can impair their sexual and reproductive functions. But, regardless of the severity, all forms of this practice compromise the physical integrity of their bodies. "External observers" are often accused of disregarding the experiences of circumcised women who report still being able to enjoy sexual pleasure and have children (Erlich 1990:152). We indeed possess many pleasure points, but this doesn't mean we should therefore stop demanding the abolition of such practices.

Like many traditional practices, it has become challenging not only to understand the metaphysical, cultural or religious reasons behind FGM, but also to justify its persistence in a dramatically different sociocultural landscape. An engineer from Hal Pulaar, Soninke, Susu or Somali background, whether living in Africa or Europe, who marries a woman from his region who has been excised or infibulated, may lack a frame of reference for understanding the practice. He might defer to the women in his family – his mother, aunts and sisters – considering it a women's matter. Culturally, FGMs are seen as part of the rituals that define femininity within a social structure designed for women. The role these practices play in socializing children, forming a female ethnic identity, and marking adulthood for women is often stressed. However, closer analysis reveals that women, who perpetuate these practices themselves, are upholding a system designed and enforced by men and the wider community to exercise control over women's bodies, sexuality and fertility.

4.4 Women's Bodies: Sites of Protection and Control for Reproduction

Female sexuality is often protected, controlled or even exploited across most cultural systems. The stakes of this are enormous. Genital mutilation is one method of controlling women's sexual desires and behaviors. This practice involves "closing" young girls to preserve their virginity and prevent pregnancies, effectively imposing a behavioral code that shapes them for marriage.

FGM is not unique to African societies, though it is most practiced there. It also occurs in Yemen, Indonesia, Malaysia and, less frequently, in India and Pakistan. In Europe, certain

surgical procedures that alter women's genitalia are criticized, despite claims that they restore health and enable a
more "normal" life. Catherine Nisak, in the 1986 issue of
Enfants d'abord, discusses adrenal hyperplasia, a condition
causing the clitoris to grow excessively (excessive by whose
standards?), resembling a small penis. In the nineteenth century,
the "correction" involved "tucking in" the enlarged clitoris to
normalize its size and appearance. The procedure, however,
was most often performed on girls to prevent masturbation.
This procedure was prevalent in the early twentieth century and
only faded in the 1950s. In the United States, until 1937, this
generated a profitable market for "orificialists" who excised
girls for masturbating. Today, vaginal reconstruction, which
costs around 1,000 US dollars, involves removing the clitoral
hood and tightening the vaginal opening to address low sexual
desire. Naturally, this makes natural childbirth impossible, and,
during intercourse, the woman must always remain beneath
the man. In the 1980s, certain publications advocated for the
excision and infibulation of young Black and Hispanic girls who
lived in housing projects to decrease the rate of teen pregnancies.
In the Middle East and North Africa, hymen restoration is still
performed in preparation for marriage. All these examples serve
to show the extent to which women's sexuality is also controlled
in cultures outside Africa.

Where does this need to control women come from? Women
are primarily viewed as bearers of the lineage; if not wives, they
must at least be mothers. In some cultures, a woman must demonstrate her fertility before marriage. Her body is governed by
cultural, religious and moral norms that dictate sexual behavior
and connect biological reproduction with social reproduction
(Matthieu 1985). Sexuality, a fundamental aspect of personal
development, is more heavily regulated in women's lives than
any other element. Even with significant social changes, fertility
remains to this day a critical marker of adulthood. Men and
women are considered adults only when they have "procreated."
But the rules of social reproduction differ between the men and
women, throwing into relief their unequal balance of power. As
numerous studies have shown, the differences between the male
and female sexes hinge less on biology than on fertility. Male
dominance, supported by both traditional and modern African
family laws that recognize men as family heads, is enforced by

controlling women's fertility and, by extension, their bodies, during their reproductive years.

It is often suggested that this dominance exists only in patriarchal systems. However, it is forgotten that in matriarchal systems, it is the uncle or brother who is the head of the family. The control over women's fertility through cultural practices – such as marriage, polygamy, forced and early marriage, dowries, early pregnancy, circumcision and the mourning rituals for women – alongside the domestic responsibilities assigned to women, and the acceptance of these practices as the norm by both men and women, expose the deep-seated sexual inequality embedded in the social and political fabric, which is perpetuated across generations. This control wanes or disappears when a woman reaches menopause, as her body ages and her reproductive capabilities cease. At this point, sexual relations often no longer exist for women, while men may continue to be sexually active with partners who can be 20 to 40 years their junior. It is also during this phase that women often regain considerable moral authority within their families, particularly over their children, driven by the age hierarchy.

It is clear, then, that women's subordination stems largely from control over their bodies, with genital mutilation being a significant aspect of this control.

4.5 Abolishing FGM: An Issue of Fundamental Human Rights, Sexual Rights and Women's Empowerment

A review of the literature on this issue shows that the debate has largely revolved around a few key questions. The first concerns the notion of bodily integrity: Is this concept universally applicable, or does its relevance vary across cultures that use body modifications like tattoos and scarifications as identity markers? Cultural relativity also raises significant questions: Should FGM be judged according to the norms of the cultures that practice it? Can the international Convention on the Rights of the Child be used to combat the mutilation of girls? Is it possible to apply this Convention universally across all societies? Does criminalizing FGM effectively deter the practice?

At another level, when it was recognized that fighting discrimination and inequality should also aim to build or strengthen women's empowerment, the concept of power itself sparked extensive redefinitions and debates. How can we talk about power for those who possess little and must devise strategies to expand their scope of action? How do we discuss autonomy and control over their own bodies in cultural contexts where total authority is automatically assigned to men? Can power exist for someone who does not control their own body, their time or the products of their labor, who is not free from the control of others (father, brother, husband, group, society) and does not enjoy social recognition of their power? These conditions pose significant challenges for women who are consistently under guardianship.[13] We must not overlook that fundamental human rights for women include the ability to make their own decisions or act independently, enjoy equal access to material and moral support and equal opportunities in the social, economic and political spheres, as well as the ability to develop their full potential, exercise their rights and contribute to the development of others.

Senegal has formally committed to the principle of equality, as underscored in its National Report to the Beijing Conference in 1995:

> Article 1 of the Constitution asserts that all individuals are equal before the law, without discrimination. Article 4 prohibits any act of discrimination, irrespective of its origin or purpose, and mandates harsh legal penalties. Article 7 states that any violation of the gender equality principle should lead to the nullification of the offending legislative, regulatory, or private act. Whenever fundamental human rights are discussed in the constitution, the terms used are individual, person, or citizen, intentionally avoiding gender distinctions. This demonstrates the government's dedication to ensuring gender equality in Senegal. (*Report of the Fourth World Conference* 1995:10)

However, an examination of legislative texts and development policies reveals that true equality has yet to be fully realized, with numerous challenges persisting. Reproductive rights, like sexual rights, are the result of ongoing struggles led by women from across the world, including feminists from both the Global North and South. These rights were further reinforced at major global conferences at the end of the last century, including the

Earth Summit in Rio (1992), the World Conference on Human Rights in Vienna (1993), the Cairo Conference on Population and Development (1994), the Copenhagen Social Summit on Poverty (1995) and Habitat II in Istanbul (1996). At these conferences, the focus on women's uteruses as central to population policies was acknowledged and, despite considerable opposition, there was a consensus on providing "universal access for women throughout their life-span to a full range of affordable health-care services, including those related to reproductive health care, which includes family planning and sexual health, consistent with the report of the International Conference on Population and Development."[14]

To be sure, several obstacles stand in our way: governmental inaction; the pressure of political, cultural and religious ideologies; and the impact of structural adjustment policies on healthcare funding. Religions – Judaism, Christianity and Islam – strive to influence current debates on sexuality and reproduction, family planning, the use of sexual protection (this was addressed at the Imam conference in Senegal funded by the United Nations Population Fund [UNFPA]) and abortion (which the Vatican opposes). The action plan that came out of the Cairo Conference on Population and Development was achieved through a difficult process of consensus-building among these diverging viewpoints. Nonetheless, it marked a significant victory for women by communicating two essential ideas:

- The first idea is that the term "population" encompasses living beings (men and women) whose various needs must be met throughout their lives.
- The second idea is that sexuality and reproduction are as vital as the right to vote or to have a job. Sexual rights are human rights.

For African women, the concept of sexual rights extends beyond the right not to be discriminated against based on sex. It includes fundamental rights such as the refusal to accept rape and incest, the right not to be married as a child – for example, at nine years old – the right to prevent early pregnancy, the right not to receive only half the inheritance left to a brother, or to be treated as property (*donn* in Wolof) to be passed down upon the death of a spouse. Essentially, it is about the right for all individuals, both women and men, to have bodily autonomy and to have control over their sexuality and fertility.

4.6 The Political and Legislative Frameworks Needed to Abolish Sexual Mutilation

The national and international context offers a wide range of political and legal opportunities that African women still under-utilize. I will highlight just a few of these.

Since their independence in the 1960s, all nations have embraced the Universal Declaration of Human Rights (1948), which prioritizes ratified international agreements over national laws (Article 79). They have also generally endorsed and ratified the principles of the International Bill of Human Rights, the African Charter on Human and Peoples' Rights (1981), and, most significantly, the Convention on the Elimination of All Forms of Discrimination Against Women (1979). This convention bolsters the Charter's provisions and other international agreements aimed at eliminating discrimination against women in both the public and private sectors. During the United Nations Decade for Women, from 1975 to 1985, and later at the 1995 Beijing Conference, strategies, action plans and programs were developed. Although these resolutions were sometimes accepted, contested, negotiated, amended or annotated to indicate reservations, they continue to be pivotal in discussions on women's rights worldwide and particularly in Africa. These documents serve as the legal foundation for addressing many concerns related to women's rights. Preparatory conferences in Nouakchott, Lusaka, Arusha and Dakar, leading up to the Beijing Conference, established African platforms that, despite numerous reservations on contentious issues, marked a turning point in promoting women's rights.

International forums of the 1990s, including those held in Rio, Vienna, Cairo, Copenhagen, Istanbul and Rome,[15] continued to advance the recognition of women's roles, needs and rights. Even in situations where national governments fail to prioritize these issues, women can leverage these international frameworks for support. For example, the Declaration and Program of Action adopted at the 1993 World Conference on Human Rights in Vienna declared that:

the human rights of women and the girl-child are an inalienable, integral and indivisible part of universal human rights. The full and equal participation of women in political, civil, economic, social, and cultural life, at the national, regional, and international levels, and the elimination of all forms of discrimination on grounds of sex are priority objectives of the international community.[16]

In December 1996, the predominantly male Parliament of Kenya narrowly rejected, by one vote, a law that would have abolished FGM. Meanwhile, other nations, facing both domestic and international pressures, have adopted more accommodating stances that unfortunately fall short of completely abolishing this practice. Often, political leaders maintain a cautious and ostensibly neutral position. But their silence typically signifies either indifference, tacit approval of such practices, or a reluctance to decisively oppose and eradicate them.

The issue of FGM was first raised not by government bodies, but by women's activist groups, who, with support from NGOs and international organizations, launched awareness campaigns within socially accepted limits. Initially, there was no push for specific legislation. However, as discussions progressed, it was suggested that existing laws should be reviewed to identify provisions that could potentially be used to challenge these practices.

Senegal maintained a cautious and ambiguous position on FGM. In the mid-1996 drafting of the Women's Action Plan (1997–2001), discussions on enacting anti-FGM legislation were particularly challenging, both in small committees primarily composed of women and in larger mixed-gender plenary sessions. Despite widespread support from the ministry, it required the perseverance of a small group to ensure that penalties for mutilations were included. Most participants, coming from other government bodies and NGOs, belonged to ethnic groups that didn't practice circumcision, and hence had limited information on the issue and no strong opinion. There was a widespread call for patience and gradual change to avoid upsetting traditional and cultural norms. This sentiment was echoed by President Abdou Diouf at the opening of the Inter-African Committee on Traditional Practices Affecting the Health of Women and Children (IAC) symposium on those traditional practices. While his very presence lent support to the fight against FGM, it did not lead to the establishment of specific legislation for its abolition.

In 1996, a significant workshop in Casamance, Senegal, brought together officials from administrations and NGOs across eight regional countries to share experiences and improve strategies to curb harmful traditional practices affecting women's health.[17] While the participants stressed the influence of cultural taboos, the lack of public awareness and the insufficient mobilization of resources, they specifically called out the "lack of commitment" from governments, noting the absence of both logistical support and an institutional framework for eradication efforts. The workshop proposed intensifying educational campaigns across various social spaces such as schools, community centers and media, targeting both the general populace and professionals in administration, healthcare and education. Key figures such as religious leaders, lawmakers, elected officials, public relations agents, artists, social workers, law enforcement officers, healthcare workers and educators were identified as crucial to the effort. Additionally, they advocated for "the adoption of laws specifically banning FGM and aligning national legislation with international conventions on the rights of women and children's rights," which all African countries have signed and ratified. Following this conference, the Senegalese Ministry of Health launched a region-wide prevention campaign against FGM with the World Health Organization's support on April 28, 1997. Despite these efforts, a formal, widespread governmental stance on legal measures is still pending, although some local successes have been encouraging. For instance, in June 1997, Malicounda, a Mandeng Muslim village, officially abandoned the practice, with local circumcisers throwing away their knives in the presence of the imam as a symbolic gesture.

Few countries have enacted criminal laws against the practice. When reviewing legislative measures taken in Africa, only countries such as Sudan (1946), Egypt (1958–9), Guinea (1957), Ghana (1994), the Central African Republic (1966) and Burkina Faso (1996) have implemented laws. However, these laws represent significant historical milestones in the ongoing fight against FGM.

Sudan enacted a law in 1946 prohibiting the severe form of FGM known as infibulation but continued to allow excision as a cultural practice. Despite its ratification in 1957, this law was largely ineffective. A similar situation occurred in Egypt: a 1958 ban was quickly undermined by a 1959 ministerial resolution that permitted partial clitoridectomy if a woman consented and the procedure was medicalized. Activists' efforts to completely eradicate FGM faced significant challenges, notably in 1997 when an Egyptian court overturned a government ban on these practices. Religious leaders supported this ruling amid widespread protests. In Gambia, a campaign initiated by the Ministry of Health and Social Welfare in March 1997, following recommendations from international health organizations including the WHO, UNICEF and the UNFPA, was undermined by a government directive issued in May 1997 on television:

> The broadcast of Radio Gambia or Gambia Television of any program that might appear to oppose FGM, or that seeks to describe the medical risks associated with this practice, is prohibited ... newspaper articles written from the standpoint of opposing this practice are also banned. Gambia Television and Radio Gambia must always support FGM, and no other program against the practice may be aired.[18]

Burkina Faso took significant steps against FGM in 1996, becoming one of the latest countries to enact abolition measures. Despite previous efforts, including threats of excommunication by Catholic organizations, families continued to practice excision on teenage girls on the eve of their weddings. The movement against FGM gained momentum in the 1960s during the United Nations Decade for Women and received substantial support from President Thomas Sankara in 1983, who oversaw the creation of the National Committee to Fight the Practice of Excision as an official body in 1990. Extensive awareness campaigns were launched, funded by organizations like UNICEF, the UNFPA and several international cooperation agencies from France, the USA, Canada and the Netherlands, as well as NGOs such as the Population Council and OXFAM. These included educational talks, radio and TV programs and press articles. The National Committee to Fight the Practice of Excision in Ouagadougou as well as provincial committees were well equipped, and an SOS-Excision hotline was established to prevent FGM and support victims. By 1996, Burkina Faso had incorporated legal measures into its Penal Code to prosecute parents, circumcisers and any accomplices involved in FGM.

Section II: On Female Genital Mutilation

Article 378: Any individual who causes or attempts to cause damage to the integrity of a female's genital organ through total ablation, excision, infibulation, desensitization, or any other means, shall be punished by imprisonment for a term of six months to three years and a fine ranging from 150,000 to 900,000 francs, or either penalty alone. In cases resulting in death, the term of imprisonment shall be five to ten years.

Article 379: If the offender is a healthcare or allied professional, the penalties prescribed shall be increased to the maximum allowable under this section. Additionally, the court may impose a prohibition on practicing the profession for up to five years.

Article 380: A fine of 50,000 to 100,000 francs shall be levied against anyone who, being aware of the offenses described in Article 378, fails to report such knowledge to the appropriate authorities.

However, it should be noted that Section III of the Penal Code pertains to the prohibition of abortion. This suggests that full autonomy over one's body and fertility has not yet been achieved.

In Senegal, as the result of pressure from women's movements and human rights organizations campaigning against violence toward women, there is an emerging discussion about the type of legislation to adopt within the ongoing reform of the Penal Procedure Code. The public's attention has been drawn to several cases of homicide and rape of women and girls from 1994 to 1997, and amplified thanks to activists' efforts, including organizing campaigns and marches, meeting with the press and with other groups, and issuing international appeals. Notably, the 1994 case of Doki Niasse, who died after sustaining injuries from her husband's abuse, initially ended with his release due to insufficient evidence. This case sparked a significant public debate on violence against women. More recently, the case of Fatou Dieng, who endured 22 years of violence from her partner, ignited another major public debate led by the same activist groups. During the trial in April 1997, the husband was sentenced to eight months in prison for assault, the maximum penalty under the law at that time. The minister of justice, troubled by the leniency of the sentence, appealed. In the current Penal Code reform, it is proposed that violence against women be considered an aggravating circumstance. This reform could potentially pave the way for legislation against FGM as well.

4.7 Conclusion

When it comes to FGM, we cannot afford to wait for time to solve the problem. A more assertive approach is needed – one that provokes a shift in collective consciousness and challenges deeply rooted traditions, sparking some kind of change, even if that change initially begins slowly.

It is clear that merely discussing FGM in terms of reproductive health and its medical complications is no longer sufficient. Despite the significance of these health issues, they do not address the broader social control imposed on women's bodies. Similarly, framing the practice in terms of cultural and religious values – such as attributing symbolic value to the act through a minor incision or any other symbolic act or ceremony of entering womanhood – falls short. Blaming any single religion, like Islam, is misguided since these practices also take place within Christian communities and other religious groups and vary even among adherents of the same faith. The lesson here is to empower women to challenge oppression justified by religious or cultural traditions. Culture and religion, while central to personal identity, should not justify the suppression of women's rights.

To my students from Africa, Europe and America who are worried about losing their feminine identity with the decline of socialization processes and rituals like excision, I feel compelled to express my refusal to accept an identity formed through oppression and domination. Identity is an ideal we construct, and as we approach the end of the twentieth century, it is crucial for African women to define it for themselves. Women have a long history of advocating for change in terms of rights – rights to equality, freedom, health, education, employment, resources and political power. The right to control one's body and sexuality is just as fundamental. Law serves as a tool to uphold these rights and should be made accessible to women.

5

Who Owns Women's Bodies? (2021)[1]

At this conference on "Sexual and Reproductive Health in the Global South" (Marseille, 2021), the opening remarks by Aurélie Gal-Régniez, Executive Director of the French NGO Equipop, on the genealogy and current challenges of the concept of sexual and reproductive health and rights (SRHR), set the stage for what follows, which is centered around this key question: "Who owns women's bodies?"

5.1 Why Ask This Question and How Do We Address It?

This question has always been present in my mind throughout my career as a sociologist and a women's rights activist.

Initially, my academic research led me to focus on women's studies at a time when I became aware of their place across all facets of sociology, which is my field; such subjects were barely represented in Senegalese curricula and scarcely more so in the francophone world. Although I managed to teach courses on family and gender relations at Cheikh Anta Diop University in Dakar (UCAD) from 1992 to 2000, using them as a gateway to women's studies, I was never able to incorporate these subjects into the official curriculum.

During my time at the University Paris–Diderot (CNRS), from 1998 to 2007, I honed my research skills and understanding of these matters, despite the challenges of integrating gender studies and feminist critique into academia, fields that continued to be marginalized during the late 1990s and early 2000s. Allow me to offer just one example: In July 2005, the General Commission for Terminology and Neology, placed under the authority of the French prime minister, issued a "recommendation concerning the French equivalents of the word 'gender.'" It claimed that "there was no linguistic need for substituting 'genre' [gender] for 'sex,'" arguing that "the expansion of 'genre' to include this meaning was unjustified in the French language."[2]

From an activist standpoint, always interwoven with my academic career, both in Africa and globally, I chaired a research network on reproductive health in francophone Africa (1992–6). In this context, I co-directed a francophone adaptation, for African readers, of *Our Bodies, Ourselves*, initially published by the Boston Women's Health Book Collective (1970). Our edition[3] featured discussions between doctors and social scientists. I also collaborated with the international feminist network Women Living Under Muslim Laws (WLUML) whose research and advocacy focus on the impact of Muslim laws (known as Sharia) on women, particularly with regard to their sexual and reproductive rights. At the Council for the Development of Social Science Research in Africa (CODESRIA) in Dakar, Senegal, a group of feminist researchers and I initiated debates leading to the creation of an annual institute on gender in 1994. This effort enabled me to develop a feminist critique of social sciences in Africa. I directed institutes on gender studies with young African researchers and published some of our work (notably, this occurred *outside* academia, with no support from the nearby University of Dakar). The last institute I led in 2011 culminated in the publication of a collective volume, *Genre et fondamentalismes* (2018), which explores cultural and religious fundamentalisms in contemporary African societies. Additionally, for over 30 years, I have been a member of DAWN, a feminist research network from the Global South (Asia, Latin America, Africa, the Caribbean) focused on development alternatives, based in Suva, Fiji. I've participated in numerous discussions about the socioeconomic positions of women in their national, regional and global contexts, emphasizing health and sexuality as critical political issues.

The question of "who owns women's bodies" isn't just a professional matter for me. I've reflected on this through my own experiences as an African woman born, raised and working in Africa. My concerns have centered around the contexts, histories and values that turn the female body into an object of appropriation targeted by various agents, sites and forces.

My remarks here focus on women's sexual and reproductive rights from a feminist perspective – one whose critique is, out of necessity, interdisciplinary. I understand that the feminism I express, shaped by my African and Black identities, is increasingly viewed with apprehension in our contemporary contexts. In the Americas, its intersectional approach, which incorporates "race" as a key analytic category, is perceived as politically dangerous. In France, the issue is often entangled in debates around *woke* and/or *cancel culture*, imported from the United States and seen as equally contentious. In West Africa, and particularly in my home country of Senegal, it is dismissed as a dangerous – even scandalous – import of Western ideology because it is seen as un-African.

5.2 "Who Owns Women's Bodies?" The Central Role of Sexuality and Fertility Underlying the Question

Sylvia Tamale, a legal scholar from Makerere University in Kampala, Uganda, offers a valuable definition of sexuality that highlights the various areas it encompasses: "Sexuality is intricately linked to practically every aspect of our lives: to pleasure, power, politics and procreation, but also to disease, violence, war, language, social roles, religion, kinship structures, identity, creativity" (2006:89).

All these aspects intersect and create normative frameworks through socialization, providing mechanisms used to control women's sexuality and fertility by employing cultural and religious rules that are often sanctioned by political authorities.

Sexuality is the arena where male and female relationships play out, and where women's strength and/or subordination finds expression. We know that the status and perceptions of women are "socially constructed" (a claim that has now become contentious); we need not cite Simone de Beauvoir to recognize that women are shaped by culture, religion and politics. Analyzing these relationships and the interplay between cultural, religious and political influences frequently sparks fierce debates among individuals in Africa, both between men and women and within groups of women themselves. Discussions about women's bodies, and particularly their sexual and reproductive health, are often viewed as challenges to the core values of their cultures and their (African) identities, which are underwritten by religious and political norms.

5.3 Femininity in Pre-colonial African Cultures: Exploring Matriarchy, Matrilineality and Motherhood as Core Symbolic Values

Rooted in pre-colonial Africa, these representations are claimed as part of women's history, one that posits matriarchy as the foundation of societies, giving women a prominent role. Cheikh Anta Diop, the preeminent theorist in this field, explored this idea extensively in his works from 1954 and 1959. Building on his theories, several African women scholars have further embraced matriarchy and motherhood as central frameworks for understanding women's historical significance and dominant roles. Following Ifi Amadiume's influential publications from 1987, 1990 and 1997, Oyèrónké Oyéwùmí continued to explore these themes in her first book and subsequent articles. In "Abiyamo: Theorizing African Motherhood," she writes: "Motherhood occupies a special place in African cultures and societies. Regardless of whether a particular African society displays a patrilineal or matrilineal kinship system, mothers are the essential building block of social relationships, identities, and indeed society. Because mothers symbolize familial ties, unconditional love, and loyalty, motherhood is invoked even in extrafamilial situations that call upon these values" (2003:1).

The importance of matrilineal lines in transmitting material, cultural and symbolic value, along with political power, is well established and beyond dispute. However, I won't delve deeply into this topic here. Instead, I'll briefly highlight a few revered "mothers" in our national history, such as Sokhna Adama Aïssé Thiam, mother of Cheikh Oumar El Foutiyou, founder of the Tukuloor Muslim Empire; and Sokhna Mame Diarra Bousso, mother of Cheikh Ahmadou Bamba, founder of the influential Mouride brotherhood.

We can trace a long history of representations of women across political and religious contexts, centered around the concept of motherhood. The Virgin Mary, revered as the Mother of God in Christianity, is a clear example of this. However, despite women's influential roles in transmitting material wealth and political power, they have historically been barred from achieving supreme authority themselves – male royal titles like *Dammel, Buur, Brak, Teeñ, Almaami, Seriñ*, among others, are cases in point.[4] This exclusion persists even when women are not part of the governing elite. If I am emphasizing motherhood, it is because of its ubiquity as a reference that sanctifies the body – or, more precisely, the womb – of women.

Colonial rule disrupted the institution of matrilineality and its structures across Africa at multiple levels, while maintaining motherhood as a central value in family and society, in line with its own ideological positions. The colonial state "afforded women limited roles within its new political structure" (Boahen 1987). The colonial education provided to women, which was granted later than that for men, primarily prepared them to be good wives and mothers, rather than educating them for professional roles. Regarding the perception of the body of the African woman, a Black body, we can turn to Delphine Peiretti-Courtis' 2014 thesis defended at the University of Aix-Marseille, in France, titled "*Black Bodies and White Doctors: Between Race, Sex, and Gender. Knowledge and Representations of the Bodies of Africans in French Medical Sciences (1780–1950)*." This work explores the deep-seated racial and sexual biases that portrayed these bodies as dominated and confined to a femininity envisioned by colonialism: heterosexual, reproductive and monogamous. This ideal promoted heterosexuality and monogamy as dominant values and relegated women to a domestic sphere defined by a strict public/private divide. The control over public space was further emphasized by scholars like Amina Mama (1997), Sylvia Tamale (2004) and Penda Mbow (2005). Barbara Rogers (1981) and Jessica Horn (2005) discussed this as not only a domestication of women but also a broader trope of domesticity that isn't unique to African women. Colonial legislation reinforced these domestic roles, granting men exclusive authority over their wives and children within the family. African women were primarily targeted by maternal and child health programs intended for married women, which were prevalent throughout the colonies.

In independent West African countries today, the cultural, religious and political landscape has not fundamentally changed the ideology that underpins women's status. Indeed, these forces continue to work together to control women's bodies, albeit in more nuanced and subtle ways, due to the influence of feminist movements and recent social changes.

In response to the questions "Isn't my body mine?" or "Shouldn't it belong to me?" it is clear that a woman's body is not entirely her own. It is confined and defined by a complex web of sociocultural, religious, political and legal norms. These include evolving African values (which never remain static), remnants of Western colonial models, the impacts of globalization, and international conventions that are ratified but not consistently enforced by our national governments. This framework is also shaped by religious doctrines from local religions, including many different faiths such as Islam, Christianity, other African churches, and Evangelical communities. Global media and social networks influence it.

Regarding sexuality and fertility, the modern African state has perpetuated the colonial practices of managing and controlling women. A feminist critique of sexualities and identities reveals how "the discourses, norms and practices of heterosexuality, centrally anchored in male authority, are emerging or have hardened into the central basis for defining personhood, gender and sexuality" (Salo and Gqola 2006:3–4).

The sexual and reproductive health of women urgently needs to be understood as a rights issue due to the persistent discrimination that affects it. Women's advocacy in Africa and around the world has prompted most West African nations to adopt various international conventions and the Maputo Protocol, albeit with some reservations. In Senegal, for instance, Law No. 2005-18 enacted on August 5, 2005, focuses on reproductive health. However, neither the Strategic Plan for Sexual and Reproductive Health of Adolescents and Young People in

Senegal (2014–18) nor the National Strategy for Equity and Gender Equality (2016–26), which promises "universal access to sexual and reproductive healthcare," explicitly addresses the sexual and reproductive rights of individuals, particularly women. The control exerted over the sexual and reproductive health of girls and women remains one of the most critical areas of discrimination they face.

In a survey on youth sexuality, the Strategic Plan for Sexual and Reproductive Health of Adolescents and Young People in Senegal recognized that the motives for engaging in sexual activities include curiosity, experimentation, need satisfaction, self-pleasure or the pleasing of a partner, imitation, poverty, influence from parents or peers and the need to prove masculinity. Yet, without any additional commentary, it reports that:

> Some young people view sexual activity outside of marriage as reckless, promiscuous, and indicative of a lack of self-control. They acknowledge the importance of upholding traditional sexual values, such as maintaining a young woman's virginity, fidelity, and abstinence, considering these practices viable options "when possible." For some, adhering to these norms is "a good thing," particularly because they are "recommended by religion" and contribute to a woman's "respectability." (Strategic Plan 2018:17)

Inequality between men and women is reflected in the hierarchies of age and gender embedded in the structure of the family and reinforced by rules that govern all aspects of a woman's life, from her sexual conduct and use of contraceptives to her marriage, fertility decisions and even her freedom of movement or personal decisions. Traditionally, women needed their husband's or parents' authorization to obtain official identity documents, choose employment, travel abroad or make legal decisions for their own children. These restrictions were stipulated in the 1972 family code, which was amended in 1984 to grant more freedoms. Women's use of contraception historically required legal permission from their husbands and the moral blessing of religious leaders, who were regularly consulted by family planning programs. Abortion is not permitted in cases of rape or incest and is restricted to situations where the mother's life is at risk, as allowed by Islam. However, the approval process is lengthy and cumbersome, leading to widespread clandestine abortions with devastating impacts on women's health. Advocacy for abortion rights remains limited, spearheaded by groups like the Association of Senegalese Women Jurists, the Association of Women Physicians of Senegal, and Siggil Jigeen (Wolof for "Uplift Women"), despite some political efforts toward decriminalization. "The state created the Task Force to buy time, signaling to society that they are seeking a 'solution amenable to all parties'" (N'Diaye 2019).

Motherhood extends beyond simply wanting children; it is often seen as a social and religious obligation. Society expects women to fulfill what is considered their "natural" role. Infertile women are marginalized because they do not contribute to the large families that men are expected to have to affirm their masculinity and social standing. This male prestige relies heavily on controlling women's bodies, whose sexuality and fertility are dictated by each community's social norms: remaining chaste, undergoing circumcision, being subject to surveillance, managing dowries, adhering to marital obligations, submitting to their husband's desires, proving their fertility and following strict widowhood rituals such as shaving their heads, wearing specific clothes, avoiding mirrors, living in seclusion and abstaining from sexual relations. Other practices like levirate and sororate marriages further reinforce these forms of control (Sow 2018).

The expectation of reproduction can deepen women's subordination, as they are shaped by social, ideological and religious pressures to continue the physical lineage of their community, often at great cost to their own health. Typically, infertility or the absence of pregnancy is blamed on women, who internalize this blame and experience significant stress and emotional strain as a result. They bear the burden of perceived failure, and, after trying various treatments, they usually let a family member or doctor discuss the issue with their husband.

It is worth scrutinizing what is often referred to as the "high fertility" of African women. French President Emmanuel Macron's controversial statement at the G20 Summit in Hamburg in July 2017, where he remarked, "when countries still have seven to eight children per woman, spending billions of euros will stabilize nothing," ignited fierce debates about perceptions and realities of fertility rates in Africa. By 2050, it is projected that 25 percent of the global population will be African. This rapid population growth in Africa is often framed in the West as a cause for concern, invoking fears of a "great replacement" by a predominantly Black African population, especially during election campaigns or socioeconomic crises in France. These fears prompt calls for African women to have fewer children. Conversely, Africa views its growing population as an asset, proposing strategies to leverage this growth. In an interview in *Libre Afrique*, Felwine Sarr, author of *Afrotopia*, encourages African governments "to invest in education due to the young demographic and pyramidal population structure. Investing in the human beings that make up this vital human resource, this reservoir of intelligence, is critical for Africa's advancement" (March 15, 2018).

Mabingué Ngom, a Senegalese demographer and prominent voice on population issues due to his role at the United Nations Population Fund (UNFPA),[5] disputes the idea of overpopulation in Africa. Asked about his perspectives on African demographics, he claimed: "Many overlook the fact that as life expectancy increases, the African population is aging. Additionally, despite the rapid pace of urbanization, the continent is not on the verge of overpopulation. Some countries, like Angola and Namibia, remain relatively sparsely populated" (2019).

To capitalize on Africa's demographic dividend, Ngom calls on the international community to leverage it to propel the continent's growth by 2050. He argues that "this demographic dividend, if effectively managed, has the potential not only to accelerate economic growth but also to enhance stability and security across the continent" (2021). He points out, though, that "achieving the demographic dividend is contingent on reducing maternal mortality, lowering fertility rates, and eliminating gender-based violence, underage marriages, and obstacles to women's access to family planning" (2021).

There is a significant debate surrounding this approach, primarily because it fails to acknowledge the crucial role of women's bodies in producing the demographic dividend. African women have not widely adopted the feminist position of being the decision makers regarding if, when and with whom they have children, a position that is often derided. Despite this, the demographic dividend is dependent upon their bodies and poses substantial health risks, not to mention challenges in navigating conflicting personal goals. Women are often blamed for declining birth rates, a global concern as populations fail to replace themselves; yet these women staunchly advocate for control over their reproductive choices. Does the high fertility rate attributed to African women significantly limit their freedom due to social and religious pressures to reproduce?

The HIV/AIDS crisis in the 1980s dramatically exposed the challenges women faced in negotiating safe sexual practices with their partners.[6] This issue underscores broader aspirations for controlling sexuality to prevent sexually transmitted diseases and to manage fertility through contraception. These are central concerns in ongoing debates about citizenship, cultural norms, gender equality and reproductive rights.

Despite numerous challenges, women's and feminist organizations have successfully pushed African public discourse toward acknowledging individual rights, freedom and responsibility concerning these sensitive issues. This shift, driven by new generations, is reshaping gender power dynamics across Africa. Currently, women face a resurgence in social conservatism and religious orthodoxy that promotes chastity and sexual abstinence (over safe sex) as state methods to combat HIV/AIDS. This conservatism is supported internationally, evident from the "Gag Rule" policies of US administrations from Reagan to George W. Bush and positions held by the Vatican and some Islamic states against international conventions promoting women's sexual freedoms. The 2003 Additional Protocol on Women's Rights under the African Charter on Human and Peoples' Rights, adopted in Maputo by African Union leaders, advocates for extensive women's rights related to sexuality, fertility, abortion, female genital mutilation, polygamy, early marriages and pregnancies, and physical and sexual violence, which are framed as issues of women's health.

This is perhaps the moment to briefly address the complex issue of homosexuality, which is present in every country and culture but is often viewed negatively by African public opinion. Homosexuality remains a crime in most African states, except in South Africa, which became the first country globally to recognize sexual orientation as a constitutional right. This decision, however, has faced challenges and a backlash. This is a significant concern for activist groups:

> Leaders within the African state and in civil society have often evoked the notion of culture, both to defend the hegemonic hold

of heteronormative gender relations as anchored within dominant notions of masculinity, and to silence any nascent claims by those who self-identify as homosexual, bisexual or transgender persons – even though, for instance, cross-dressing has a long history in parts of Africa. (Salo and Gqola 2006:3–4)

5.4 Conclusion

We should take seriously Patricia McFadden, a feminist sociologist from Swaziland, who argues that we need to move beyond the sexual comfort zones established by culture and religion. In many of her writings on sexual health and sexual rights for African women, McFadden argues that women are facing a critical moment shaped by religious and cultural norms surrounding sexuality and fertility. They are confronting entrenched taboos that have compromised their health and sexual autonomy, regardless of age or social class. These taboos must be questioned. Cultural conformity, often masquerading as African authenticity, serves to uphold male sexual privilege at the expense of women's bodily autonomy.

To do so, we need to rethink our approach, finding the courage and determination necessary to address the "crisis of sexualities."

6

Religion and Politics in Sub-Saharan African Secular States (2014)[1]

6.1 Introduction

The place of Islam in sub-Saharan Africa, where the majority of the population is Muslim, has been a crucial political issue both before and after the region's countries gained independence in the 1960s. The subject has been extensively researched, with historical, political, religious and sociocultural perspectives offered on various countries, including Senegal, Nigeria, Cameroon, Chad, Burkina Faso, Côte d'Ivoire, Sudan, Tanzania and South Africa.

The long-standing presence of Islam stems from an early Islamization that left its mark on what has rightly been described as "Islam in African," or even "Islams of Africa" (*Afrique politique*, 2000). From Islam, these diverse societies appropriated its creed and ideologies, its discourses, norms and practices, allowing it to take root as a faith shaped by the rich and varied local traditions of religiosity, belief and spirituality. Over time, Islam became a power force in (re)shaping both individual and collective identities, (re)organizing many territories and political formations, and acting as an ongoing source of cultural and historical vitality. It also served as a means of self-affirmation and as a way to legitimize resistance to colonial domination, articulated and channeled by political and social organizations as well as by religious brotherhoods. The Muslim history of sub-Saharan Africa – unfolding on both local and global scales – has given rise to a substantial and complex body of research, both African and international. While it is impossible to summarize this work here, it remains essential to keep it in view when examining the contemporary forces at play.

It is well known that colonial powers adopted different approaches – ranging from control and confrontation to circumvention and assimilation – toward the agents, institutions and sociocultural and religious systems they dominated. It bears recalling, as a telling example, that the French imperial state adopted secularism with several "accommodations." For instance, while the French applied the Napoleonic Civil Code – which could not be imposed on the local populations – there was also an allowance for a "customary" system that respected local rules and norms, a prime example being the Islamized Wolof customary laws in Senegal. Conversely, the British Empire's policy of Indirect Rule allowed local Muslim (such as emirs and sultans) and traditional leaders (such as Ibo and Yoruba rulers) to enforce their laws, provided they adhered to principles of "justice, equity, and propriety," terms commonly expressed in colonial times.[2] These varied approaches significantly influenced how different regions interpreted and implemented secularism, which is the subject I am exploring here.

In the French colonial context, significant effort was directed toward enforcing secularism, as mandated by the 1905 law that separated church and state. Initially, the administration struggled to enforce the Napoleonic Civil Code, established in 1804 in the context of a Christian society, on the Muslim societies in North and West Africa. These societies displayed vehement resistance, insisting on maintaining their religious laws for personal matters such as marriage, divorce and inheritance, and wanted these issues handled in Muslim courts established for that purpose. Despite secularism being a formal part of the institutions, it was constantly challenged and was a subject of negotiation regarding its application, leading to conflicts between the centralized state and the people it sought to govern. Since 1792, the French government recognized only civil marriages, which had to precede any religious ceremonies, but as a colonial authority, it failed to enforce this policy among Muslim populations. For them, the religious ceremony was the only recognized form and took precedence, without entailing any civil commitments between spouses.

In the 1960s, as African nations gained independence, the significant influence of Muslim leaders within their communities (whether they were in positions of power or not) led newly appointed African leaders to adopt various strategies for managing or suppressing resistance. For instance, Guinean President Sékou Touré actively fought against the influence of the Almaami[3] in Fuuta Jallon, a predominantly Fulani region that adhered to its version of Sharia law. On the other hand, Senegalese President Léopold Sédar Senghor adeptly managed his relationships with leaders of religious brotherhoods through a combination of control, cooperation, bargaining and clientelism.[4]

The late 1970s saw the emergence or resurgence of an identity-centric Islam, whose discourse was gaining traction around the world, and which was seeking to align itself with state power. This movement in sub-Saharan Africa was marked by a rise in activities from organizations and reformist groups advocating for new practices. This led to debates about whether these changes represented a "renewal" or a "reinterpretation of Islam" (Coulon 2002). It appears to have been a combination of both. Reflecting on the rapid expansion of this movement, Muriel Gomez-Perez notes, in the introduction to her book *L'islam politique au sud du Sahara. Identités, discours et enjeux*, that:

> Since the 1980s, a perspective within the Muslim community has emerged arguing that Islam is not outdated but rather a powerful tool for bringing the continent out of isolation, engaging the public sphere and challenging state authority. This perspective marks the rise of political Islam, which has become a means to claim new spaces and advocate for a system of reference rooted entirely in the sacred, countering the secular systems established by states since gaining independence. (2005:13)

This repositioning of Islam and its religious forces within the political realm of government, where secularism stood as a rule of governance, transformed secularism into a target for attacks ranging from criticism to outright rejection, depending on the situation. This shift was part of a broader dynamic that was unfolding.

Mauritania declared itself an Islamic state in July 1991. Algeria, Western Sahara, Mali and Senegal border this West

African country. Gaining independence from France in 1960, Mauritania has a predominantly Muslim population, including various ethnic groups such as Arab-Berber Moors who were elevated to positions of power by the French colonial administration. In 1991, Mauritania established Islam as the state religion and Arabic as the official language. Without going into the details of Mauritanian history, we can note that both internal dynamics and geopolitical considerations influenced this shift in governance. The policy of Arabization strengthened the control of Arab-Berber Moors over Black African populations from the Senegal River Valley (Soninke, Hal Pulaaren, Bambara, Wolof), who do not identify with Arab culture. In a society where slavery was only abolished in 1981, the Islamization of laws introduced complications, especially for the *Abid* (slaves) and *Harratines* (descendants of freed slaves),[5] with former slave owners demanding compensation. The fight against slavery has been criticized by some groups as anti-Islamic.[6] By adopting Arabic and declaring itself an Islamic Republic, Mauritania aligned itself more closely with both Maghreb nations (Morocco, Algeria, Tunisia, Libya and Egypt), where Islam is the state religion, and the Middle East, cementing its membership in the Arab League.

Political motives have also driven attempts to Islamize governance and laws in countries like Somalia and regions such as Northern Nigeria. Since gaining independence in 1960, Somalia has faced many severe political crises, starting in 1969, leading to the country's fragmentation as well as interventions by US troops, the United Nations, and neighboring nations such as Ethiopia and Kenya. Islam has been exploited as both a pretext and a tool in conflicts between various warlords. From June to December 2006, the Union of Islamic Courts, established in 1993, sought to establish an Islamic regime. Today, the federal government, established in August 2012, is undermined by armed Islamic militias, including Al-Shabaab. In the Federal Republic of Nigeria, the debate over Sharia (Suberu 2005) has polarized the political class since independence, revealing a divide between the predominantly Muslim North and the predominantly Christian South. According to Suberu, "the Sharia controversy is also complicated by the ambiguous and contentious nature of Nigeria's secularity" (2005:212). Referencing Ali Mazrui (2001), he speaks of a "Shariacracy," a term used to describe the situation.

Today, this debate has largely receded, overshadowed by Boko Haram's explicit ambitions for expansion. The Islamist group's military incursions have destabilized not only northern Nigeria but also neighboring countries – Cameroon, Chad and Niger – with its aim to impose Muslim law across the country and the wider sub-region. These developments highlight the complex relationship between politics and religion in sub-Saharan Africa. The debates emerge from situations that illustrate, on one hand, that "Africa has not experienced the decline of religion or the rise of secularization that many predicted would come with modernity. Instead, religious beliefs and practices have been revitalized in Africa, growing stronger and intensifying. This has led to more complex relationships between society, politics, and religion" (Mame Penda Ba 2012:9).

However, these examples also underscore the reality of secularism as a constitutional principle, a concept that has evolved significantly from the colonial era through to independence (Mbow 2008). Unlike in North Africa, most African countries do not have Islam as their state religion. Typically, political institutions and legal frameworks avoid relying on religious sources, reserving them mainly for family law due to the Muslim majority in their populations. While the constitution prohibits any discrimination based on sex, race or religion, and bars political associations founded on these distinctions, the family code provides citizens with options guided either by civil principles or by religious clauses. Therefore, inheritance laws may follow a civil model, which ensures equal distribution among heirs, or a Muslim model, which allows for unequal distribution between men and women in the division of assets.

For the purposes of this discussion, it is worth focusing specifically on the challenges secularism faces in regions with a deep-rooted and significant Islamic presence. Currently, secularism is either under pressure or at risk in societies that are experiencing profound changes due to a variety of factors: the ongoing process of Africanization and a growing allegiance to markers of identity, "modernization" of economies and political systems, rapid urbanization, and the pronounced effects of globalization. In this context, there is a growing concern about how these factors collectively impact the civil rights of women.

6.2 The Impact of Religion and Politics on Women's Citizenship

For the sake of this discussion, when I use the word "secularism," I am referring to the French practice of *laïcité* rather than its Anglo-Saxon iteration, which lies outside the scope of this study. The focus here is on two countries that adopted their secular approach from their French colonial past. Secularism has a rich and varied history across France and other European countries, influenced by different circumstances, visions and political practices. It is challenging to condense this history, but it is essential for supporting my argument. For instance, in France, secularization was "an emancipation effort against a Church that, due to France's tumultuous history, had assumed a hegemonic (and sometimes monopolistic) role in the symbolic realm," Baubérot argues (1990:216). In debates on secularism in 2004 – a year marked by significant social tensions in France, including Islamic radicalization and controversies over the wearing of the headscarf in public and school settings – Baubérot, who specializes in this subject, explained: "According to legal standards, secularism [*laïcité*], for me, seems to be based on three fundamental principles: the protection of freedom of conscience and worship; the prevention of religious dominance over the state and civil society; and the equal treatment of all religions and beliefs, which includes the right to disbelieve" (2004).

For the philosopher of French secularism, Henri Pena-Ruiz, we should take note of two crucial ideas in the same vein. The first idea declares that "secular emancipation demands that religions completely disengage from public power, which entails a strict separation of two distinct realms, rather than the suppression of one to favor the other" (1998:64). The second asserts that "the secular ideal is about upholding a standard, not a cultural variable that is relative and context-specific" (1998:69).

The constitutions of nations that were once French colonies clearly reflect a continued commitment to secularism. This point is emphasized by Robert Deni Segui, an Ivorian law professor who specializes in the constitutions of African francophone countries (2010). He reminds us that, for the Republic of Côte d'Ivoire, "the republican form and the secularism of the state may not be subject to revision" (Art. 127). Chad calls itself a "sovereign, independent, secular, social, one and indivisible republic." It explicitly guarantees "the separation of religion and the state" (Art. 1). Following significant political turmoil, the Central African Republic adopted a new constitution in January 1995, repealed it in 2003, amended it in 2010, and later introduced "Law No. 13.001 on the Constitutional Charter of Transition" in 2013. All these frameworks continue to promote the same principles, with the Central African Republic affirming that "the Central African Republic is a sovereign, indivisible, secular, and democratic rule of law" (Art. 18). It even explicitly bans "all forms of religious fundamentalism and intolerance" (Art. 8). The major political crisis that began in March 2013 alarmed officials, as it seemed to be provoked by underlying tensions between Muslim and Christian communities, although the motivations for this crisis are, in fact, more complex.

A few anglophone countries explicitly state their commitment to secularism in their constitutions, such as Tanzania, which claims: "The United Republic is a democratic, secular and socialist state" (Art. 3). This stance is influenced mainly by Julius Nyerere's vision, which guided the country to independence. Another example is the Gambia, which declares itself a "sovereign secular Republic" (Art. 1), despite its preamble starting with "In the name of God, the Almighty." Despite this legal framework, most of these countries do not traditionally uphold strict secularism. Moreover, their constitutions commonly reference God in the preamble: "Swear in the name of God swear – So help me God" (Constitution of Sierra Leone 1991); "May God protect our people" (South Africa 1996); "For God and my country" (Constitution of Uganda 2005); "Acknowledging the supremacy of the almighty God of all creation" (Constitution of Kenya 2010). As is the case in the UK,[7] these nations focus more on protecting religious freedom rather than enforcing secularism. For instance, Uganda and Kenya clearly state they do not endorse a state religion ("Uganda shall not have a state religion": Art. 7; "There shall be no state religion": Kenya, Art. 8). However, all of them uphold the principles of freedom of religion and conscience, and prohibit discrimination based on religion (South Africa, Art. 15; Uganda, Art. 32). Some constitutions even guarantee the "freedom to change [one's] religion or belief" (Sierra Leone, Art. 24). Specifically, Tanzania's constitution affirms that "Every person has the right to the freedom to have conscience, or faith, and choice in matters of religion, including the freedom to change his religion or faith" (Art. 19).

Despite its various interpretations and inherent contradictions, secularism remains a focal point in political discourse as it embodies a "sociopolitical mode of organization." As Baubérot explains, "it is a major sociopolitical matter within any society, setting the terms by which social life will be defined and contested" (2014:2). Indeed, secularism, regarded as a "universal societal project," has become a pivotal element in modern debates about democracy. Western societies brandish it as a principle of democracy, especially when evaluating its applicability in countries with differing ideologies and religions, particularly Islam (Sow and Pazello 2014:185).

Considering the challenges of secularism, we would do well to reflect on the philosopher Ghaleb Bencheikh's question on whether contemporary societies have truly chosen to "desacralize human life" (2005). The answers to this are uncertain and often ambiguous. Not only do political and religious powers continue to maintain close ties, but political elites frequently stray from secular norms by openly invoking religion and religious figures within what are supposed to be secular frameworks. Additionally, governments often adopt positions that could be perceived as religious on sensitive issues such as sexual and reproductive rights, including sexual freedom and orientation, fertility control, abortion and the prevention of sexually transmitted diseases like AIDS (Sow and Pazello 2014).

The secularization of laws has long been a battleground between religion and politics. This process is vital for women's citizenship because it helps liberate them, to varying extents, from the clutches of religious ideologies. Religions such as Islam, Judaism and Christianity base their teachings on foundational texts, which include rules and norms that have frequently been contested and that dictate gender relations and women's roles in society. Notably, religious leaders from these faiths made their opposition felt during the major conferences of the Decade for Women (1975–85), where they opposed the Beijing Platform's measures as contrary to their moral beliefs. As Henri Pena-Ruiz reminds us: "For women, the secularization of law – its detachment from the literal interpretation of a sacred text that many scholars argue reinforces and seeks to immortalize the biases of a patriarchal society – is the key to their emancipation" (2003:260).

The UN itself has implemented measures that have influenced women's rights. In February 2006, at the meeting establishing the Human Rights Council, the 56 countries of the Organization of the Islamic Conference (OIC) proposed a recommendation on "the defamation of religions and prophets [...] which is incompatible with the right to freedom of expression, as it leads to violations of human rights." This group included 18 countries from sub-Saharan Africa. The organization intended to denounce in this way the notorious Muhammad cartoons, which were a contentious issue in Europe at the time. It tasked the Council with "promoting universal respect for all religions and cultural values" and "preventing cases of intolerance, discrimination, and incitement to hatred and violence [...] against religions, prophets, and beliefs." They also urged countries to fight against any racist and defamatory actions toward religion and religious adherents. Renewed by the OIC in 2007, 2008 and 2009, this recommendation resulted in a resolution passed by the Council in 2009, sparking strong reactions from many civil society organizations. The organization Women Living Under Muslim Laws (WLUML) strongly criticized the recommendation in a statement:

Ahead of the vote, hundreds of seculars, religious, media, women's and other groups from around the world appealed to the Council in Geneva to reject the proposals, which the 56-nation OIC introduced. Civil society groups have expressed that the "combating defamation of religion" Resolution may be used in certain countries to silence and intimidate human rights defenders, religious minorities and dissenters, and other independent voices. In effect this resolution has the potential to dramatically restrict the freedoms of expression, speech, religion and belief. Item 12, which "*Underscores the need to combat defamation of religions by strategizing and harmonizing actions at local, national, regional and international levels through education and awareness-raising,*" can be used to silence progressive voices who criticize laws and customs said to be based on religious texts and precepts. Furthermore, this Resolution will have a disastrous effect on national laws in several countries that already stipulate they will comply with international treaties on human rights only if they do not prejudice laws said to derive from Islam. (April 23, 2009)

Under pressure from the international community and the United Nations, the Council finally dropped the concept of "defamation of religions" in March 2011.

To frame this discussion on secularism in sub-Saharan Africa, I have selected three countries as examples. Although these countries are influenced by strong religious ethics and morals that impact their legal systems, they have not established Islam as their state religion. It is useful in this context to distinguish between "secular" and "secularized" states. For the sake of clarity, "secularized" states can be understood as those where legal institutions include elements of religious law, specifically Islamic law, as observed in the three countries under discussion.

6.3 Sudan: A Secular or Secularized State, with Sharia Law as Its Legal Framework

Sudan, a nation deeply rooted in Muslim traditions since the fifteenth century, gained its independence in 1956, transitioning from its status as Anglo-Egyptian from 1899 to 1956. While its post-independence history is marked by numerous regime changes and bloody political and armed conflicts, the country has consistently been engaged in intricate legal debates. Notably, 20 percent of Sudan's population, predominantly residing in the southern regions, was Christian. The constitution has always upheld and continues to maintain freedom of religion.

During the colonial period, Sudan depended on three distinct legal systems: Common law governed civil transactions; Muslim laws addressed personal status issues for Muslims; and customary laws applied to other religious and ethnic groups, especially those in the South (Badawi 2008:217).

After independence, Sudan was quickly divided over whether to recognize all existing customs – including the practice of Islam – as diverse legal sources, or to establish Islam alone as the singular legal framework for all Sudanese, regardless of their faith. The 1973 constitution chose a hybrid approach, declaring that both Muslim law and traditional customs would jointly serve as the foundation of law (Art. 9). However, following a military coup in 1983, the new government unilaterally extended Islamic law to cover all legal areas, though it stopped short of declaring Islam as the state religion. This legislative shift reignited conflicts with the non-Muslim south from May 1983 until May 2004. Roland Marchal notes that this move clearly demonstrated a strategy of identity-based power consolidation:

> Right from the start of the nationalist movement, the call for an Islamic constitution was used more as a tactical tool in the rivalry among equally Islamic parties than as the core identity issue the Islamists portrayed it to be. Thus, Sharia is primarily a political rather than an ethical issue, concerning decisions about citizenship rather than safeguarding Islamic values and social interactions, which no political group aims to dispute. (2004:31–2)

The Interim National Constitution of the Republic of the Sudan of 2005 stated that "nationally enacted legislation having effect only in respect of the Northern states of the Sudan shall have as its sources of legislation Islamic Sharia and the consensus of the people" (Art. 5-1). One section of the constitution (Art. 6) was reserved for religious rights:

> The State shall respect the religious rights to:
> (a) worship or assemble in connection with any religion or belief and to establish and maintain places for these purposes,
> (b) establish and maintain appropriate charitable or humanitarian institutions,
> (c) acquire and possess movable and immovable property and make, acquire and use the necessary articles and materials related to the rites or customs of a religion or belief,
> (d) write, issue and disseminate religious publications,
> (e) teach religion or belief in places suitable for these purposes,
> (f) solicit and receive voluntary financial and other contributions from individuals, private and public institutions,
> (g) train, appoint, elect or designate by succession appropriate religious leaders called for by the requirements and standards of any religion or belief,
> (h) observe days of rest, celebrate holidays and ceremonies, in accordance with the precepts of religious beliefs,
> (i) communicate with individuals and communities in matters of religion and belief at national and international levels.

Despite the threats posed by an authoritarian government, civil society and human rights organizations continued to engage in discussions and voice concerns about the adverse impacts of the radicalization of Islamic law on society. At a conference titled

"Legal Reform in Sudan," organized in Khartoum in 2006 by the Ahfad University for Women (Omdurman, Sudan), along with the United Nations Mission in Sudan and the United Nations Institute for Peace, human rights and women's rights advocate Zeinabou Abbas Badawi presented on the much-needed reforms to Sudan's Muslim and customary family laws, exposing the inconsistencies and discriminatory practices against women. As a response to these practices, the "Rights of Women and Children" section of the 2005 constitution declared that:

(1) The State shall guarantee equal right to men and women to the enjoyment of all civil, political, social, cultural and economic rights, including the right to equal pay for equal work and other related benefits.
(2) The State shall promote woman rights through affirmative action.
(3) The State shall combat harmful customs and traditions which undermine the dignity and the status of women.
(4) The State shall provide maternity and childcare and medical care for pregnant women.
(5) The State shall protect the rights of the child as provided in the international and regional conventions ratified by the Sudan.

But what did this look like in practice? Despite articulating gender equality in Article 21 of the 1998 constitution and Article 32 of the 2005 constitution, Sudan never signed CEDAW, although it ratified several other human rights conventions, including the African Charter on Human and Peoples' Rights of 1993. Badawi notes that all constitutions seem to tell women that they are granted equality, but if religion dictates otherwise, their hands are tied (2008:221). She also stressed that merely changing the existing Muslim personal status laws was ineffective without simultaneously reforming other laws – such as those concerning access to employment and economic resources – addressing educational and health concerns, and combating cultural biases against women. She believed it was especially crucial to appoint more female judges to ensure that women could feel confident and believe in the integrity of the justice system.

These discussions highlighted a dire situation for women, exacerbated by amendments to the family code that introduced stricter Muslim legal provisions. The 2010 report from the Organisation for Economic Co-operation and Development

(OECD), *Gender Equality and Social Institutions in Sudan*, criticized these reforms for curtailing numerous freedoms. Notably, the reforms toughened divorce procedures to deter women, upheld polygamy and marital authority, and mandated that, in the event of divorce, custody would pass to the father once boys reached age six and girls age eight. Additionally, they perpetuated gender disparities in inheritance, failed to address the lack of laws addressing violence, continued female genital mutilation, limited access to land and financial resources, and enforced a strict dress code for "decency." The case of journalist Loubna Ahmed al-Hussein, who was sentenced to 40 lashes for wearing pants, brought international attention to these issues. According to the Sudanese Penal Code, Article 152, anyone who "commits an indecent act, offends public morals, or wears indecent clothing" can be subjected to 40 lashes (*Le Monde*, December 8, 2009).

To resolve the protracted armed conflict between the North and the South, Sudan was required to implement democratic reforms following peace talks mediated by the United Nations. These talks culminated in the Comprehensive Peace Agreement of 2005. A referendum held in January 2011 eventually led to the secession of the South. During this period, President Omar El-Bashir announced the intensification of Sharia law in the remaining parts of the country. This was a significant blow for many women's groups who had hoped the peace talks would provide an opportunity to push for legislative changes, especially regarding Article 149 of the Criminal Act. This article, dealing with rape and sexual violence, often resulted in impunity due to stringent definitions and the requirement for evidence. In a country with multiple conflict zones, rape had become a weapon of war, particularly in Darfur. In 2008, REDRESS, an organization dedicated to fighting torture, published a damning report on these violent acts.

In June 2007, the *Law without Justice* report highlighted the failure to acknowledge rape and its repercussions, resulting in perpetrators escaping punishment and victims being left without support. Moreover, these victims are at risk of suffering further abuse, as they can be accused of adultery if they fail to prove the rape. An unmarried woman convicted of adultery (*zina*) is subjected to 100 lashes, while a married woman could face the death penalty. The report mentions that in February and March

2007, two women were sentenced to death on charges of adultery (Fricke with Khair 2007:7). A campaign initiated in January 2010 by Salmmah Women Resources Center, Mutawinat, and other local women's organizations, with backing from the WLUML Network and Refugees International, lost momentum when President El-Bashir was indicted by the International Court of Justice a few months later. Several of these groups, including the Salmmah Women Resource Center, were dissolved without trial.

We can see the impact, then, of enforcing conservative laws on the civic rights of women. This issue was stressed by the women's associations leading the campaign, as noted in their final campaign report:

> The status of women in the Sudan, as in many Arab and Islamic countries, relies on family and social relationships, and their citizenship opposes and clashes with the family institution. They are also still subject to sex, masculine mediation and power, physical and moral subordination to the patriarchal family, alleged and imaginary gender roles, and unrealistic and inhumane social assumptions. Therefore, we find that the legislative achievements, amendments and legal reforms have touched the laws governing the status of both sexes in the public sphere, while the law governing women's status in the private sphere is not only impervious to change, but also to amendment and reform. (Hashim et al. 2011:3)

6.4 Mali and Senegal, Secular States: A Turn Toward Sharia or Conservative Politics?

Mali and Senegal, both former French colonies, became independent in the 1960s, as part of the Mali Federation, but separated shortly thereafter. They inherited the same legal system from their colonial past, incorporating customary laws that governed private matters into their postcolonial legislation. Both nations were significantly Islamized between the seventh and eleventh centuries and have predominantly Muslim populations, ranging between 80 and 90 percent. Despite this, they also have vibrant Christian communities actively participating in society.

Although Islam continues to exert significant influence in both the social and political spheres, both Mali and Senegal deem themselves secular states. Mali's current constitution, first adopted in 1992 and revised in 1999, "solemnly pledges" in its preamble "to uphold the republic's form and the state's secularism." Senegal's constitution, last amended in June 2009, states in Article 1 that "the Republic of Senegal is secular, democratic, and social." It is noteworthy, however, that the 2001 constitution, known as the "Constitution of Alternance,"[8] omitted the term "secularism" and described the nation as "a political, economic and social democracy." Mali's constitution also emphasizes, in its preamble, "the commitment to defending the rights of women and children" and states in Article 2 that "all Malians are born and remain free and equal in rights and duties. Discrimination based on social origin, color, language, race, gender, religion and political opinion is prohibited."

In their constitutions, both countries have formally committed to the Universal Declaration of Human Rights, adopted on December 10, 1948, and to the African Charter on Human and Peoples' Rights from June 27, 1981. Additionally, Senegal's constitution acknowledges its commitment to the Declaration of the Rights of Man and of the Citizen from 1789, along with international treaties enacted by the United Nations and the Organization of African Unity. It has ratified several key human rights documents, including the Convention on the Elimination of All Forms of Discrimination Against Women from December 18, 1979, and the Convention on the Rights of the Child from November 20, 1989.

In Mali, although women's rights are not explicitly mentioned, Article 119 of the constitution ensures that "all existing legislation remains valid as long as it does not contradict the provisions of the current constitution or has been explicitly repealed." Furthermore, historian Bintou Sanankoua notes that: "Laws that are contrary to the letter and spirit of the constitution, as well as to the international instruments mentioned in the preamble of the constitution and which form part of the constitutional framework, should be declared unconstitutional. This, in principle and theory, guarantees family rights" (2008:5).

These details in the legal texts are crucial as they reflect the advancements enshrined in the constitution. The current Senegalese constitution has made substantial strides in terms of gender equality. Not only does it ensure equality for all under the law, regardless of gender, but it also explicitly guarantees in several sections that:

Art. 7: "All individuals are equal before the law. Both men and women have equal rights. The law actively supports equal opportunities for both men and women to hold public offices and positions."

Art. 15: "Both men and women have equal rights to own and acquire land, as specified by law."

Art. 17: "The state and public authorities are obligated to protect the physical and moral well-being of families, with particular attention to disabled and elderly individuals. The state ensures that all families, especially those in rural areas, have access to health services and overall well-being. It also specifically guarantees women, particularly those in rural settings, improved living conditions."

Art. 18: "Forced marriage is a violation of individual freedom and is both prohibited and punishable according to the law."

Art. 19: "Women have the right to own property independently from their husbands and to manage their assets personally."

Art. 22: "Every child, boy or girl, throughout the country has the right to attend school."

Art. 25: "Discrimination based on sex regarding employment, wages and taxation is strictly prohibited."

Art. 60: "At least two-fifths of the Senate must be composed of women."

Women's organizations have frequently argued that many provisions of the family code and other regulations contradict the constitution. For instance, while Article 7 asserts that "men and women have equal rights," the family code continues to position the man as the head of the household, a provision rooted in Islamic tradition.

Laws concerning rights have improved, and this progress is undeniable. These advancements result from the efforts of women in Africa and globally, who often face backlash due to conservative social norms. These societies, deeply influenced by a long-standing tradition of Islamization, are now experiencing the rise of political Islam, which has led to a resurgence of fundamentalist and far-right religious movements, such as Wahhabist, Salafist and Ibadou Rahmane groups, further complicating the situation. Alongside this, there has been an increase in religious associations (female *dahiras*), and the media's portrayal of Muslim women promotes highly conservative norms, urging them to wear "decent" attire such as veils and discouraging physical contact with men, including handshakes. Many cultural practices are increasingly viewed through a religious lens. Campaigns to abolish female genital mutilation in Senegal, for example, have been resisted with arguments linking a woman's purity to excision; unexcised women are deemed impure and unfit for cooking or sexual relations. Despite the legal ban of this practice in 1999 in Senegal and other West African nations, the issue remains sensitive and is rarely discussed openly. The revival of religion, with its call to return to "core" cultural values, aligns with a global trend of reverting to national cultures under the guise of protecting cultural rights.

The family codes in Senegal and Mali are telling in this regard. These are the only laws that incorporate Muslim-inspired provisions. They largely uphold the inequalities between men and women inherent in religious teachings, consistently positioning the man as the head of the family. Interestingly, the efforts to revise these codes, a major initiative of women's organizations, have led to various outcomes, some of which are completely at odds with each other.

The revision of Mali's 1962 family code became its own debacle, as several local and international organizations have pointed out. After years-long revisions involving the government, civil society groups and religious associations, a new code was introduced and approved by the National Assembly in mid-2009. However, this sparked wide protests by Muslim groups, leading to days of rioting in the streets of Bamako and other areas. Several provisions of the new code faced intense opposition due to religious (Islamic) and cultural objections:

Art. 281: "Marriages must be secular; all religious marriages need to be officially registered with the civil registry."
Art. 282: "The legal minimum age for marriage is set at 18 years for both sexes."
Art. 311: "The law requires mutual respect between spouses, replacing the previous requirements of the wife's obedience and the husband's protection."
Arts. 556 to 573: "Parental authority is now defined collectively, rather than being solely the father's responsibility."

President Toumani Touré's government swiftly withdrew the code for further review. At the end of 2011, a new version that undermined these advancements was introduced and passed, to the great disappointment of women's organizations and grassroots activists. The statement issued by the International Federation for Human Rights (FIDH), the Malian Association for Human Rights (AMDH), the Space for Exchange and Consultation of Women of Mali, and the Inter-African Union of Human Rights (UIDH) expressed the concerns of women's organizations in Mali and across the continent about protecting the human rights of Malian women. Their letter to President Toumani Touré expressed their deep disappointment: "Several provisions in the new code conflict with the constitution's non-discrimination principle. For instance, Article 311 now stipulates that 'a woman must obey her husband,' and Article 314 designates the man as the sole head of the family. Additionally, Article 282 establishes the legal marriage age at 16 for girls and 18 for boys."

Other organizations pointed out that in matters of inheritance and divorce, it is now the head of the family who resolves these issues, either through customary practices or by drafting a will under civil law. Religious marriages performed in mosques are now legally recognized, whereas the previous code had excluded this provision because it did not fully protect women's rights.

The current demands of rebel groups in Northern Mali will further complicate this notable decline in secularism and the debates it sparked. As of March 2012, these groups are insisting on the strict enforcement of Muslim laws in the territories they control. The threat to secularism has intensified due to a severe political crisis that has been disrupting the country since 2012. This crisis is connected to events occurring across North Africa during the same period. The long-standing issue of "Tuareg irredentism," dating back to the independence era, acted as a catalyst for the crisis in Mali. Mali's history has been characterized by 50 years of sporadic unrest, followed by negotiations, agreements and eventual breakdowns between the state and political factions in the North. On January 17, 2012, following several violent clashes with the army, the National Movement for the Liberation of Azawad (MNLA) proclaimed the independence of Azawad as an Islamic state. This declaration was strongly backed by various Islamist groups, including Ansar Dine, the Movement for Oneness and Jihad in West Africa (MUJAO), Al-Qaeda in the Islamic Maghreb (AQIM) and Boko Haram from Nigeria. These groups were better armed than the

Malian army tasked with defending the region. Overwhelmed by the inability of state authorities to manage the situation, a coup d'état in March 2012 ended the civil government led by President Toumani Touré.

In 2012, jihadist groups took control of the entire northern region of Mali, including Timbuktu and Gao. Eventually, they ousted the MNLA from these areas and declared Sharia as the fundamental law. Due to the ineffectiveness of a transitional government established under African and international pressure, atrocities were committed against local populations. Administrative buildings were demolished, religious sites and mausoleums vandalized, and invaluable manuscripts – a part of African and global heritage – were damaged. In response, the French military operation, Serval, launched in January 2013 with substantial support from Chad and Niger, halted the jihadists' march toward the capital and their hold over the North. A new president was elected in July 2013. Although he upheld the secular principles of the republic, he began his inaugural speech with a lengthy Quranic verse. Despite these efforts, the crisis in the North remains unresolved, and jihadist groups continue to emerge, carrying out sporadic terrorist attacks.

In contrast, Senegal has undertaken a long and challenging process to reform its family codes, facing numerous obstacles along the way.

> Despite new constitutional provisions, women's calls for shared authority over the family remain unfulfilled in Senegal. Notably, under President L. S. Senghor, Senegal was among the first African nations to implement a unified family code applicable to all citizens, regardless of their faith. To be sure, this code includes provisions for polygamy, but this is one of several options: monogamy, polygamy with two, or polygamy with multiple wives. The irreversible choice of monogamy has been controversial and stirred public debate. Inheritance laws still favor men over women. However, significant progress includes the requirement that divorces be legally adjudicated. Additionally, recognizing women's contributions to household maintenance through domestic work and removing the need for marital consent to work represent important advances introduced in the 1984 revision of the code. (Sow 2005)

This issue was raised by numerous organizations, such as the "Senegalese Women Jurists." Fatou-Kiné Camara, the president of the group, pointed out in 2007 that the religious rules enshrined in the code continued to perpetuate inequalities between men and women. In 2004, women's organizations managed to avoid the implementation of a new family code. This code was not proposed by the brotherhoods, which had adapted more or less to the 1972 code, but by a new group of stakeholders. The Comité islamique pour la réforme du code de la famille au Sénégal (CIRCOFS), a committee of highly qualified Senegalese francophone and arabophone professionals (lawyers, doctors, professors, engineers), sought to reconnect with the country's religious roots. In 2002, the committee suggested a new personal status code that would apply only to Muslims. Babacar Niang, respected attorney, former head of the Bar Association, and president of CIRCOFS, noted in a press conference to present the new code in 2002 that:

> Indeed, it is necessary to adopt a new code that fundamentally differs from the current Family Code. To achieve this, we must honor each individual's freedom of conscience, which our Constitution guarantees. This can be done by replacing the Family Code with a Personal Status Code that applies personal laws specific to each individual's beliefs. Specifically, this would mean that Sharia would govern Muslims, while Christians and non-Muslims would follow their respective personal laws. (Brossier 2004:78)

The reforms proposed by CIRCOFS would revise or repeal numerous provisions in which the Senegalese legislature had set new standards due to international conventions and recognition of women's rights. These reforms would affect laws related to marriage (Book 2); adoption, parentage and child custody (Book 3); guardianship (Book 4); wills (Book 5); inheritance (Book 6); and charitable donations (*Waqf*) (Book 7). Against this backdrop, the committee proposed a markedly outdated code that ignored the 1972 legislation and the subsequent three decades of reforms. This proposed code sought to constrain options around marriage, replace judicial divorce with repudiation, limit Muslim women to marrying only Muslim men, enforce strict obedience from wives and paternal authority, create disparities between men and women in inheritance rights, deny inheritance rights to illegitimate children, and repeal the law against female genital mutilation. This would represent an unprecedented rollback of women's rights accumulated over many decades.

These new measures reintroduced clear discrimination against women, which comes as quite a shock in the early twenty-first century. They provoked widespread indignation among numerous local women's groups and from Abdoulaye Wade, the president of the Republic, who declined to put the proposal up for a vote in the National Assembly. It is essential to recognize that the family continues to be the primary arena for ongoing debates against secularism throughout the political history of the country.

Lastly, it is worth discussing a significant point of tension between the government, the political class and especially the Islamic associations. While the absolute parity law, passed by the Parliament on May 19, 2010, aligns with Article 7 of the constitution – which promotes equal access for women and men to official positions – it caused quite a stir. The political opposition was taken by surprise and was as much disturbed by the boldness of the law as by the president's unilateral decision. Islamic associations were the most vocal in their opposition, arguing that the law afforded women a level of equality incompatible with Muslim laws, despite this inequality still being present in the family code. Nonetheless, the law enabled the Senegalese Parliament to achieve 43 percent female representation after the 2012 legislative elections. The first violation of this law occurred when Touba, a religious city and the heart of Mouridism, refused to comply with the gender parity requirement in the 2014 local elections, a decision illegally sanctioned by the Ministry of the Interior.

6.5 Conclusion

The history of women's movements in sub-Saharan Africa documents diverse forms of resistance in all the struggles they have engaged in, against both colonial authorities and the Founding Fathers of Independence, as well as contemporary powers. It is to their efforts that we owe significant social advances. Currently, we are facing a period of backlash, fueled in no small measure by political Islam. As Senegalese historian Penda Mbow argues, secularism is key to understanding the relationship between Islam and democracy. She writes: "The relation between Islam and democracy is being defined by the demands from Islamists and advocates of political Islam, as well as by the necessity for a separation of powers, and thus, by the question of secularism" (2010:3).

As secularism faces challenges and loses ground politically, the strong influence of Muslim laws on family codes, and the re-emergence of debates about Islam, prompt us to examine the evolution of Islam not only as a religion but also as a force of politics and identity formation in these two countries. The resurgence of Islamic discourse from the 1970s and 1980s occurred during a crisis of modernization. Undoubtedly, this has led Senegalese and Malian Muslims to rethink and reconstruct their identities and their faith. However, reintroducing the issues of women's identity and rights into the religious sphere in Muslim societies endangers their status as citizens, a concern that North African women shared during the Arab Spring. Their status as citizens is central to the ideals of democracy and modernity, as they evolve on the continent. How can we safeguard these in the face of religious encroachments on family, political, social, sexual and reproductive rights? The rights to contraception and abortion, in particular, remain frequently challenged.

We must acknowledge that secularism is a crucial defense worth maintaining. A political analysis of the situation in Mali and Senegal reveals how the fluctuations in secularism significantly impact citizens' rights. Various discourses aim to subjugate these populations, particularly women, to a religious and cultural order, despite the democratic progress made at the beginning of the twenty-first century. For women, the struggle to reclaim their rights from political and religious institutions is central to their fight for democracy and modernity.

CONCLUSION
AFRICAN FEMINISM NOW

7

The Representation of Women and Claims to Citizens' Rights in Africa: Beyond a Political Debate (2019)[1]

7.1 A Few Questions by Way of Introduction

Representations of female identity are extremely important because they frame women's individual stories and their claims for social and cultural rights, for sexual and reproductive rights, for economic and political rights – those are the most common. Two questions arise: first, how to be a woman, claim rights and freedoms, and remain African in contemporary societies where the identity values forged by our long histories have undergone profound changes because of – most notably – colonization, decolonization and globalization? Second, how to build one's identity freely, and assume it equally freely, when norms and rules are so entrenched in culture, religion and politics, and are primarily about societal control over individuals and groups in general, and over women in particular? It is a complex process which can weaken those women whose actions are questioned or condemned in the name of these "sacrosanct" norms.

Thus, women's struggles do not fall only within the socio-political debate on gender relations, a debate which would seem almost easy to engage in. African quests for more equality, social justice and effective citizens' rights are confronted with different representations which are "in competition" with one another: the much-criticized Western models inherited from colonization and globalization; the (re)asserted African civilizational and ideological values; the religious values that are (re)claimed as cultural resources and "identity alibis" (*alibis identitaires*). African women are constantly challenged on what is considered as a Western approach in their outlook and aspirations. Whenever they oppose cultural injustices, their legitimacy is assessed by the degree of their Africanness. They are challenged on their religious identities, which are (almost) never to be questioned.

Now, how can we elaborate a more relevant approach, or more relevant approach*es*, that are acceptable to us and can help us to understand the issues that affect us? The answer is far from simple. Academic research, like many forms of action-research or pure activism, is faced with a whirlwind of ideas about the way empirical data should be collected, read, sorted and analyzed. Drawing conclusions is just as complex (Imam, Mama and Sow 1997). I have experienced this whirlwind throughout my academic career and during my fieldwork. I have faced this complexity, especially about women's issues, with more or less happiness, anxiety or suffering depending on the circumstances, the time and place where I was speaking and working. I believe most of us have experienced this.

I will attempt to briefly clarify my position as an African feminist, a position which is subject to various quandaries on the African continent. I am an African feminist, rooted in a continent which is deeply steeped in its cultures. And I do avail myself of the right to read and reread the pages these cultures have produced, and to draw past and present stories from them. I want to be able to question their shifting values (because they are alive), to analyze their realities, transformations and contradictions. Should I not appraise their multifaceted contributions to universality, in relation to time and space, in order to imagine, if not dream, their future? Our cultures are not only memories of struggle against the colonial West, the dominating West. Our cultures are also our memories and life spaces, which we reinvent every day, at every moment, with every generation. Our cultures are the fruit of our actions and constructions, deconstructions and reconstructions, conquests and defeats, etc. We need to know them and revisit them, using the critical analytical tools that have been developed over time.

When asked for a title that encapsulates the essence of this talk, I suggested "The representation of women and claims to citizens' rights in Africa." As women, we are constantly represented according to cultural, religious and political ideologies (systems of ideas) which imagine us, fantasize us or criticize us, be it as individual or collective icons. It is up to us whether we succumb to these representations and assume them, claim them or challenge them. All those representations constitute as many stakes and challenges in claiming our rights as citizens. We shall now see how.

7.2 Identity: A Social Construct

What is identity? This is a question which is widely debated among academics, politicians and activists, in the religious and cultural spheres, as is the case today. Let me just highlight one or two ideas. In his book on *The Power of Identity* (1999), sociology professor Manuel Castells defines identity as the marking, by religion, culture or any other determinant, of any individual or community to allow them to live in society. For Castells, it is essentially a social construct which "is a source of meaning and experience." Identity, as he understands it, is:

> the process of construction of meaning on the basis of a cultural attribute, or a related set of cultural attributes, that is given priority over other sources of meaning. For a given individual, or for a collective actor, there may be a plurality of identities. Yet, such plurality is a source of stress and contradictions in both self-representation and social action. (1999:6)

The relationship between gender and identity is linked to the history of the interaction between biology and culture (Löwy and Rouch 2003), which I will not discuss at length here, except to say that biological sex merely allows individuals to perform so-called "natural" functions. Beyond the biological, being a woman implies gender-based assignations – assuming a female identity (as opposed to a male identity) within the family and in society. Through these assignations, human relations are based on a set of attitudes and behaviors which are represented, if not caricatured, as signs of weakness or strength on the basis of imagined criteria which are themselves ritualized into models and values. Again, we can gather ample evidence of this both in popular literature (sayings, stories, tales, proverbs, adages) and in scholarly literature.

This leads to other questions: How can we study the processes of construction of identities and their categories? How can we dismantle the positioning mechanisms in the social hierarchies as they exist between individuals, classes, groups of all kinds, between men and women, between the elderly and the young? How can we document the multiple processes of domination/ submission, their justifications, their institutionalization in social, political, economic systems? These identity assignations (gender, age, class, language, religion, ethnicity, race, various roles and statuses…), all culturally and/or religiously endorsed, depending on their logic – one could say intersectionality – determine the standards and rules of representation that can be sources of discrimination, stigmatization, prescription, injunctions, etc. While women and their movements have long lived and suffered the consequences of these assignations, one can now witness a multipolar intensification of challenges to, and rejections of, the sexual division of social status and roles almost everywhere in the world. Women's claims as citizens generally question these representations of female identity, which, beyond politics, pose clear social challenges. What kind of society do we want? Are we going to pursue models prescribed by the social codes in force, which we try to negotiate and reimagine according to our aspirations?

7.3 Confronting the Representations of Identity

To claim something is to confront it. It is to refuse to abide by the norms, rules and decisions created and imposed by the cultural, political, moral or religious orders which vary according to our contexts. How can we achieve this?

Feminism is one way of challenging these orders, their representations of the social roles assigned to gender, and the resulting inequalities suffered by women. It allows us to analyze women's conditions and to deconstruct the mechanisms of inequality between sexes.

To be a feminist is to want to change these power relations, to promote equality in law, to encourage equal access to citizens' rights for everyone. Feminism (I should say *feminisms*) has theorized, to varying degrees, the centrality of the "oppression" of women. It sees sexism as the reason why women are oppressed, marginalized, made invisible – excluded even. Undeniably, feminist activists have taken a different approach to explaining the causes, forms and acts of sexism and the changes that have occurred in the course of history and used a different language (including gender) to understand and describe them. Gender concepts have helped us reflect about power relations between sexes. All these theorizations show that "the term feminism covers a diverse array of politics centered around the pursuit of more equitable gender relations; this is true of feminism in Africa" (Mama 2005). Amina Mama, a Nigerian sociologist whose team posts Feminist Africa, a website hosted by the University of Cape Town, continues:

> Proper documentation and analysis of the various manifestations of feminism, and the ways these have changed over time in different African contexts, is hampered by the lack of access to resources and the limited opportunities for debate, networking, and scholarship grounded in continental contexts. As a result, the debate around African feminism and feminism in Africa remains highly contested and difficult to define.

At this point I would like to introduce some African perspectives about the place of women in culture, even if these perspectives have brought as many divisions as contributions to the debate. They continue to fuel controversies, regardless of whether they relate to methodological, historical or political issues.

The perspectives of Western feminists on the "global" issue of women, with the emergence of Women's Liberation Movements (WLM) and various conceptualizations of women in the Global South, such as Women and Development and Gender and Development, between 1970 and 2000, have been widely debated by activists from other parts of the world grouped together as "the South" (as opposed to "the North"). Though dominant, these perspectives were perceived as arrogant because they had an allegedly universalist approach to the priorities, demands and strategies of struggle of other women. As such, they attracted very strong criticism. In the USA, we have witnessed the reactions of Black Feminism, which deplored the fact that the questions of race and the history of slavery were not taken into consideration in American feminist studies. As Kimberlé Crenshaw, who coined the term "intersectionality," wrote: "Because of their intersectional identity as both women and people of color within discourses that are shaped to respond to one or the other, the interests and experiences of women of color are frequently marginalized within both (sexism and racism)" (2005:54).

In a comparable setting, thinkers from sub-Saharan Africa initiated significant epistemological shifts regarding the pertinence of feminist notions and examinations. The decolonization of the social and feminist sciences in Africa was an impressive achievement (AFARD 1977). Nkiru Nzegwu, the founder and director of *JENDA: A Journal of Culture and African Women Studies*, articulated the motivation behind the journal's creation:

> Our conceptualization of *JENDA: A Journal of Culture and African Women Studies* was guided by two main objectives: the first is to create a space from which to theorize our experiences, presently marginalized in today's global context of unequal economic relations; and the second is to wrest ourselves from the mould of stereotypical assumptions in which this international economic order and its attendant culture of hierarchy have cast us. (2001)

7.4 How to Reflect on the Place of Women in African Culture and History?

Breaking the myth of the emancipation of women, often described as a "benefit" of European colonization, was the first mission of all women involved in any reflection and action on these issues. Scholars of Africa had to identify and consider the continent's own histories and values, and this was precisely the aim of the symposium on The Civilisation of Women in the African Tradition, which took place in Abidjan in 1975. Thinkers (both men and women) looked into African women's status and powers, whose origins could often be found in the matriarchal system. The debates on matriarchy as a universal system of social organization are not new. For Johan Bachofen, the well-known Swiss theorist of matriarchy (1981), "the maternal right belongs to a more ancient civilization than the paternal right," but there was a universal shift from matriarchy to patriarchy. The historian of African civilizations, Cheikh Anta Diop, however, takes the counterpoint to this theory, which implies the superiority of patriarchy, "synonymous with spiritual yearning toward the divine regions of the sky, with purity and moral chastity" (Diop 1981:27), over matriarchy, characterized by a "passive dependence on earthly life, material things and bodily needs" (Diop 1981:27). In fact, Diop argues that both systems exist in the world: "these two systems encountered one another and even disputed with each other in different human societies, [...] in certain places they were superimposed on each other or even existed side by side" (1981:25).

The presence of matriarchy as a basic social institution attests to the profound cultural unity of Africa. Diop goes on:

> Matriarchy is not an absolute and cynical triumph of woman over man; it is a harmonious dualism, an association accepted by both sexes the better to build sedentary society where everyone could fully develop by following the activity best suited to his [and her] physiological nature. A matriarchal regime, far from being imposed on man, by circumstances independent of his will, is accepted and defended by him. (1981:114)

Several theoretical approaches have been built on the importance of matriarchy and have highlighted the cultural specificities of African women in this context – see the works of Ifi Amadiume (1987, 1990, 1997), Oyèrónké Oyéwùmí (1997) or Kandji and Camara (2000), to name just a few of the more renowned scholars. All the main ideas, or the seeds of these ideas, were already present in Cheikh Anta Diop's work.

Ifi Amadiume was one of the first scholars to argue that the colonial system subordinated women whose political power was inscribed in its organizations. She rejected the gender-based nature of political power relations. Speaking of *The Invention of Women: Making an African Sense of Western Gender Discourses*, Oyèrónké Oyéwùmí had little time for gender as a concept of power relations. For her, it is only in Western culture that the "woman," because of her relationship to her body, is constructed as a category, both in relation and in opposition to "man" ... that other category. African cultures define hierarchies through social relations, not gender. There is no such thing as gendered cultural logic. One may also refer to seniority (senior–junior relations). But the most important factor is motherhood as another basis of women's power because it is the very foundation of their identity. For Kandji and Camara, the subordination of women is not universal. In Antiquity, matriarchal law made equality between sexes a fundamental value of Pharaonic societies. The woman is the source of life, hence her power. African concepts of the body emphasize only biological differences between genders; they do not speak of inequality, superiority or inferiority.

Ahmeth Diouf, a Senegalese magistrate and linguist, Jimi Adesina, a Nigerian social scientist, and Lewis Gordon, an African American philosopher of Jamaican origin, all share a common devotion for matriarchy and remind us of its importance in understanding African social facts. Ahmeth Diouf, who has worked on African maternal rights, has highlighted their evolution and their sensitive remnants in contemporary Wolof culture. Adesina and Gordon are fascinated by issues surrounding the matriarchy of motherhood, an area of research characterized by profound epistemological changes with the appearance of new terms to describe women's sexuality and fertility (motherhood, mothering, matrifocality, matricentricity). Adesina concludes:

> Finally, for African activists and scholars working for gender equity, the works of Amadiume and Oyéwùmí point to the basis for appropriating the "useful past" from a diversity of African pre-colonial histories. As Amadiume (1997:23) argued: As European feminists … seek possible ways out of their historically oppressive patriarchal family structure … inventing single-parenthood and alternative affective relationships … in the African case we do not need to invent anything. We already have a history and legacy of a women's culture – a matriarchy based on affective relationships – and this should be given a central place in analysis and social enquiry. (2010:16)

7.5 Rereading and Revisiting Human Cultures Using Critical Analytical Tools Progressively Developed over Time

Social science studies on women have compelled scholars to take part in this broad movement of decolonization, of rereading and reappropriation of sociology, culture and history by the African communities themselves. As African women, we needed to re-establish our own histories, our concealed – if not tribalized – cultural specificities. But can we not deconstruct them through new analyses when they become outdated and out of context?

How can women's claims be granted when they seem to offend the celebrated "traditions," as we usually call our cultures? The relations of seniority which, according to O. Oyéwùmí, dictate relations in African societies are necessarily power relations, whatever the sex. To rule over a family requires hierarchical relations which, as Bakare-Yusuf notes, are primarily gender relations (2003).

The need to seek and enjoy more rights has been well understood by women of all backgrounds and has led to many successful campaigns and projects which have resulted in an increasing number of competitive female entrepreneurs. These rights include, among others: the right to access land and other natural resources; the right to obtain credit without the guarantee of land, which is controlled by men at the community and state levels; the right to political participation and to achieve greater gender parity in political institutions (in municipal councils, for example); the promotion of compulsory education for girls and their access to more and more qualified jobs; the strengthening of women's economic activities.

In 2017 women made up 42 percent of Senegal's Parliament. This was achieved thanks to the struggles of the Senegalese Women's Council, which brought together women from civil society and political parties, and owing to the support of crowds of women who took to the streets whenever necessary. Many have doubted the competence of women in this realm, but never questioned the competence of the 100-percent-male Parliament in the first decades after independence. And if today some complain about the mediocrity of our Parliament, isn't this mediocrity the result of maneuvers by the fighting political classes, and of governance challenges?

Reforming the family code has been a long struggle in all countries. In Senegal, Léopold Sédar Senghor, the first president of the Republic, managed to impose a unique family code for all Senegalese citizens. He gave the judge alone the right to rule on divorce between spouses. That was a beautiful feminist victory for women, even if, unfortunately, culture still leads to discriminations. There have been many other beautiful feminist achievements: the minimum age of marriage has been redefined;

women are now able to make decisions about contraception without the approval of their husband, the marabout or the priest.

It is true that one cannot be a feminist in Africa without first identifying the African sources of sexism – the weight of patriarchy, the intersection of gender inequalities and age, class, ethnicity, caste, race, religion, sexuality, etc. Recognizing and accepting that "the body is political" is an old feminist claim that has taken into account the needs of women as reproductive and sexual rights: control of their sexuality and fertility; advanced advocacy for the right to abortion; prevention of child marriages and forced marriages; guaranteeing the physical integrity of the body (abolition of female genital mutilation [FGM]); fighting against sexual violence; criminalization of rape in families or in conflict, etc. "A child, if I want, when I want, with whom I want" is shocking language that women's control of their own fertility should nonetheless permit! Maternity, whether sublimated or imposed, has ideological, cultural and religious meanings which we must analyze more subtly and more critically.

But while it has been difficult to recognize the weight of external patriarchy (that of colonization and globalization), the move to endogenous patriarchy, which is regularly endorsed by culture and religion, has been more difficult. All of us – men and women, researchers and others – have put forward the "original" matriarchy to glorify our positions. Matriarchy is at the root of African societies, writes Cheikh Anta Diop. The woman's body is the origin of creation, which explains the power and the presence of women in matriarchal societies. We have made it our matrix of thought, even if there are hurdles along the way. If patriarchy is a proven political system that raises men to power, does matriarchy follow the same structuring patterns in history? Is it not rather a political system based on the uterine transmission of power and assets? This constitutes a huge problem because women are struggling to deconstruct patriarchy and its conjunction with other religious, colonial patriarchies. Deconstructing African patriarchal institutions strengthened by culture and religion, and endorsed by politics or religion, has been and remains a challenge, as we are grappling with deep-seated identity issues which women find difficult to question for fear of losing their identity. We could have redefined polygamy, the dowry, the wearing of the Muslim veil, handshaking, etc.

There is one last point that I would like to highlight: it is the rise of religious and cultural fundamentalisms (Sow 2018). Some call them radicalism. I call them fundamentalisms and I can witness their effects in the public space (streets, media, academic and associative spaces), in political life (because it is a threat to secularism and results in the blurring of powers – executive, legislative and judicial; there are no others, contrary to what some would have us believe and even want to impose on us). To put secularism in danger is to go back on so many of the women's rights which were conquered thanks to the many conventions and protocols we have elaborated, not thanks to holy books or some interpretation of customs.

7.6 What Conclusion?

Women's studies have evolved considerably with new theoretical developments. The sociology of the family has also renewed the study of its dynamics, its changing types of arrangement, of discussion, of negotiation, of conflictual relations between individuals. African cultures are now experiencing changing dynamics that need to be considered and analyzed with appropriate critical tools. Should we not revisit the African storytellers' and poets' feminine and maternal icon of *Mama Africa*, *L'Afrique Mère*, brandished by many of our male interlocutors in response to our discourses? They always highlight the "power" of their mothers during our exchanges on the relations between men and women in society.

How can we better understand the place of women in our societies, from the political hierarchy to grassroots communities, when it comes to their access to land, resources, political power? What is their influence in the face of the many ancient and contemporary forms of a very real and persistent patriarchal power? The debate is far from over.

8

What Secularism Means for African Women's Rights and Citizenship[1]

I join this conversation as an academic researcher in sociology and an activist, as the director of Women Living Under Muslim Laws (WLUML) and a member of several women's and civil society organizations. In both roles, I use a feminist critique to understand and analyze the status of African women in the past, present and future.

Secularism has been a critical issue for women's organizations and women's human rights defenders. Women's rights and citizenship start in the family. In societies with predominantly Muslim populations, however, it has been difficult to set up a body of family laws encompassing all citizens regardless of their faith because this is seen as contradicting Sharia "law."

I am here to say that secularism is an issue for women, as stated by Marième Hélie-Lucas, founder of Secularism Is a Women's Issue (SIAWI). Women's movements are part of the debate on secularism, as religion and culture shape women's status and rights.

8.1 Secularism or *Laïcité* Today

As a concept, secularism is rooted in various historical contexts that make it difficult to define it properly without taking history into account. We agree that secularism relates to politics and religion, but the experiences of secularism and secularization might differ from one context to the other. We can draw examples from European countries that, although they claim to share the same Christian culture, have different perspectives on secularism.

I would like to define French secularism, or *laïcité*, because Senegal and many former French colonies in West and Central Africa have inscribed *laïcité* as a basic principle in their constitutions. Without a doubt, *laïcité* refers to the separation of politics from religion. The concept of *laïcité* arose from French history. The secularization process in France since the French Revolution was "an emancipation movement confronted with a church that the tumultuous history of France had made into a hegemonic (even monopolistic) institution in the universe of symbols." The church was at the heart of political power in monarchical France – it consecrated the crowning of the kings of France.

The French Revolution abolished the monarchy. Secularism was established as a political measure with the Law of 1905 that enshrined the separation of church and state. A new government was set up where "the Republican State, as an emanation of the democratic ideal, had as its ambition the replacement of the all-embracing function of the Catholic Church in its temporal capacity" (Bencheikh 2005:113). It did not exclude religion, but proclaimed the separation of the state and religion. In France itself, there is a difference between *laïcité* and the process of laicization or secularization. French *laïcité* would be, in fact, "the political product of a historical secularization process." Secularization has also been linked to the modernization of societies.

For me, secularism mainly refers to the religious neutrality of the state in the management of the country and its politics. Laws passed in parliament in secular states should not avert or stifle free debate on societal issues by referencing "holy" principles. In most African countries, including in North African countries where Islam is a state religion, there are different ethnicities, cultures and faiths. Whenever a law is passed that is based on the principles of a leading ethnic group, culture or faith, it will inevitably marginalize or exclude minority groups.

The intervention of religion in politics is an important challenge. Most of our states establish a separation of powers to prevent one power – executive, judicial or legislative – from exercising the core functions of another. The current rise of religious fundamentalism, however, has impacted this balance of power. For instance, in Senegal people have started to refer to religious leaders as constituting a symbolic "fourth power." Religious figures have become increasingly involved in political debates and relied upon as political intermediaries. In the 1990s, cardinals and archbishops led national conferences and peace talks in Central Africa.

When Mali became divided by sectarianism in 2012, Imam Mahmoud Dicko, head of the Haut Conseil Islamique du Mali, proposed to be an intermediary during the political negotiations between the state and separatist Northern Mali movements. Yet Dicko was also the radical Muslim leader who led popular riots to force former Malian President Toumani Touré to ban the progressive family code that was passed by Parliament in 2008. The Economic Community of West African States (ECOWAS) is currently seeking the support of religious leaders to prop up peace talks in Guinea-Bissau, which is plagued by chronic political instability.

In Senegal we have also seen a gradual erosion of *laicité*. Senegal's first president, Léopold Sédar Senghor, was a Christian elected by a local constituency including a large part of the peasantry, which was predominantly Muslim. There was a separation of the state and the mosque, although Senghor maintained relationships of domination and collaboration with the leaders of Senegal's Muslim Brotherhood. President Diouf who succeeded him was not as strong a president, so he had to negotiate and share power with religious leaders. Then in 2000, President Abdoulaye Wade brought religious figures into greater political power when, after the very first democratic transfer of power in Senegalese electoral history, he went to his Marabout and thanked him for his prayers on national television.

Lastly, secularization has been described as a way to modernity in the West. As Africans, can we claim that Westernization is the sole path to modernization?

8.2 Religion, Culture and Politics

While women's movements in Africa have tried to promote new social contracts that advance social justice and gender equality, they have faced continual backlash by those who seek to revive religious and cultural values that hold women back. While secularization of the law has helped to promote women's rights – especially after 30 years of major international summits and accords on women, the environment, human rights, populations and more – these achievements continue to be challenged by many ordinary people and fundamentalist groups.

State and religious authorities across Africa maintain close ties. This mingling of religion and politics has become evident in public debates around sexual freedom, contraception, abortion, AIDS prevention, sexual orientation, same-sex parenting and bioethics (euthanasia, medically assisted conception, genetic testing, cloning, stem cell research, etc.). These questions pose moral challenges to individuals' identity and religion.

They also illustrate the interplay between religion, culture and politics, including the:

- *acculturalization of religion*, which I understand to be the cultural dimension of religion, or various practices that are cultural and not religious, such as female genital mutilation, banning women from driving, or wearing a burqa;
- *religionizing of culture*, or when culture is used in the same way as religion to define identity; and the
- *religionizing of politics*, which I take from Karima Bennoune, an American–Algerian law professor, who uses this term to explain the use of religion for political purposes.

Karima Bennoune, a law professor at University of Michigan Law School, described the religionizing of politics in her analysis of US President Barack Obama's first visit to Cairo:

In his celebrated 2009 Cairo speech, US President Obama laudably aimed to reach out a much-needed hand of friendship to Muslim-majority societies across the globe. However, his embrace of a confessional worldview in that address was worrying. Speaking to those gathered at Cairo University, the President focused not on citizenship, or national or regional identities, but solely on presumed religious identities, thereby casting Muslims as a sort of monolithic bloc of people who are defined by their religious belief. In addition, he repeatedly quoted from religious texts. This article asks how using such a religious lexicon in political discourse affects the separation of religion and state. It also argues that religionising politics unwittingly plays into the hands of funda-mentalists. (2013)

Increased religious radicalism among all faiths is reshaping the relationship between religion and politics. Religious groups are being imbued with a "mission" to lead society and to transform social contracts, which is based on a very specific view of the sacred and which may diverge from the original interpretation of their religion. Many of these religious groups want to impose a society that is completely based on conservative religious norms, which they themselves define.

8.3 Secularism and Women's Rights

Secularism does not transform the gendered nature of religions. But it has to address it. In the birth of modern nation states, religion went out of the public sphere, but it never left the personal and individual sphere. It remained in the realm of family, of communities and of religious institutions, which are constantly the basis for creating and recreating political power.

Religious institutions often provide spaces and social networks that the secular state has not been able to provide. In Muslim societies, brotherhoods and dahiras (faith-based organizations where women organize religious events) offer a space for commu-nities to help each other and collaborate. As a result, there is a false division between the public sphere and the private domain. Compounding this dynamic is the critical role religious institu-tions have played and still play in the provision of health and educational services throughout Africa.

Also, some countries have carved out space in the law for the imposition of religious dictates concerning the family, which impacts women's rights the most. Laws that recognize men as head of the family, that protect the indissolubility of marriage as a sacrament or that do not recognize the rights of children born outside of wedlock are all based on patriarchal religious rules that are shared among Abrahamic faiths (Judaism, Christianity and Islam).

8.4 Allowing Religious Principles to Dictate Family Laws often Means Reinforcing Gender Inequality and Control over Women's Bodies

Sharia "law" is considered fundamental for many Muslims, even though there are variations of Sharia that communities create themselves. Sharia regulates prayer, fasting, marriage, divorce, widowhood and the laws of inheritance. It includes a dress code as well as other codes of conduct. Sharia is at the center of current debates on Islam, secularism and modernity.

Muslims, whether fundamentalist or not, have always insisted on respect for Islamic values in managing male and female relations within the family. Niger and Chad do not yet have secular family codes because of their adherence to Sharia "law." The majority of Muslim countries continue to elaborate and revise their family codes in an effort to reconcile their interpretation of Sharia with reforms to modernize the law. Political leaders typically take many precautions not to hurt the spirit of the Quran.

Senegal was the first Muslim sub-Saharan African country to have implemented a secular code that applied to all communities in 1973. But this code leaves room for interpretation by citizens on many civil and religious matters. This has led to conflicts between the state and Muslim organizations that want to impose a literal interpretation of the Quran on society. Family laws are often at the center of these political controversies. For instance, efforts to end polygamy, address gender inequality in inheritances, and other matters affecting women's rights run up against the need to respect Sharia "law." Thus, in Senegal and elsewhere, there are legal provisions drawn or inspired by Sharia that have institutionalized gender inequality in state constitutions and in social codes that uphold traditionalist views about the sexual, matrimonial and social behavior of women.

Yet women's rights activists and supporters of Sharia disagree about the existence of gender inequality and discrimination. For Sharia supporters, gender inequality is not at issue, because all believers (men and women) are allegedly equal before God with no intercessors. However, in the famous verse 34 of Sura 4, the Quran emphasizes: "men are the protectors and maintainers of

women, because God has given the one more (strength) than
the other; and because they support them from their means.
Therefore, the righteous women are devoutly obedient to their
guard." So if the husband is the guard of the spouse, how can
she control her body, sexuality and fertility? This notion is what
guarantees the power of men over women in Muslim countries.

This divergence of views is why supporters of Sharia have
resisted recognizing questions of discrimination raised by the
Convention on the Elimination of all Forms of Discrimination
against Women (CEDAW). They have expressed reservations
over issues of gender equality before the law or over nationality,
marriage, divorce and inheritance issues.

At the United Nations and other international forums, religious
fundamentalists have contested efforts to address gender discrimination. Religious figures from the Vatican, as well as Mullahs
from Iran, Saudi Arabia, Sudan and elsewhere, attend international conferences on human rights to assert their views. And,
often, they weigh in on and influence decisions in women's
conferences, with the complicity or indifference of state actors.
The United States has also been complicit in allowing religious
actors to dictate foreign policy, as the Bush administration did
with the imposition of the global gag rule.

In March 2009, the UN Human Rights Council once again
passed a resolution urging member states to put laws in place
to prevent criticism of religion, specifically mentioning Islam.
Members of the Human Rights Council voted 23 in favor of
the resolution, while 11 nations opposed it and 13 countries
abstained from voting. This vote had a profound impact on
the ability of women's organizations to contest the imposition
of religious laws in Muslim countries. The resolution can now
"be used to silence progressive voices who criticize laws and
customs that are based on religious texts and precepts" (Hélie-
Lucas 2011).

8.5 Conclusion

Considering these developments, we must raise the questions:
What do religion, culture and politics have to do with my body,
and isn't my body mine? It is very important to promote a human
rights approach in which citizens, and women in particular, can

be involved in decisions and policies about their bodies. We cannot let patriarchal bodies continue to dictate women's health and rights.

At the international level, most African states have signed and ratified international human rights treaties (although the United States has not). Thus, we can cite the International Covenant on Civil and Political Rights; the African Charter on Human and Peoples' Rights; the International Covenant on Economic, Social and Cultural Rights; the Convention on Elimination of all Forms of Discrimination Against Women; the Optional Protocol and the Convention on the Rights of the Child – to advance and support women's rights on the continent. Most African states also ratified the Protocol to the African Charter on Human and Peoples' Rights on the Rights of Women. They drew plans of action from international conferences, such as the World Conference on Human Rights in Vienna, the International Conference on Population and Development in Cairo, the Women's Protocols of Beijing and others, into national programs or policies. In theory, international laws have precedence over national laws.

However, it is difficult to enforce most international treaties and bring about gender justice in the law due to opposition by domestic leaders, such as parliamentarians, and societies themselves. Thus, we must advance debate on these questions – and address resistance by religious groups – to establish truly secular states that can protect gender equality in Africa.

Notes

1 The Political Mobilization of Women in West Africa: Forms, Sites and Contemporary Stakes

1 This article is an abridged version of a contribution with the same title that served as the foundational document for the study *Gender Equality: Striving for Justice in an Unequal World*, UNRISD, Geneva, 2005.

2 The feminist movement reached a new level of prominence in the 1960s, particularly in the United States. It would later become allied with the civil rights movement, especially with the struggles of African Americans.

3 The districts are administrative divisions.

4 Jeanne Martin Cissé was an exceptional figure. In 1962, she became the first secretary-general of the Pan-African Women's Organization, established from the remnants of the Union des femmes de l'Ouest africain (UFOA) – or the West African Women's Union – whose first congress was held in Bamako in July 1959 (Ba Konaré 1993:55).

5 The year 1960 was chosen as the average date of independence for many African countries; 1975 marks the beginning of the United Nations Decade for Women.

6 The effects of these restructurings on societies in the Global South were analyzed in a research project by the Development Alternatives with Women for a New Era, or DAWN: Taylor 2000, published under the title *Marketization of Governance*.

7 The coup occurred a few weeks after the death in 1984 of Sékou Touré, who had ruled Guinea unchallenged during a severe succession crisis.

8 Data sourced from the Initial Report, and Second and Third Combined Reports, on the Implementation of the Convention on the Elimination of All Forms of Discrimination Against Women in the Republic of Guinea, November 1998, Ministry of Social Affairs, Women's Promotion, and Childhood.

9 Moussa Traoré was overthrown in 1991 following popular protests against his dictatorial regime, by General Toumani Touré, who, in an exceptional move, returned power to civilians one year after taking control. He remained President of Mali until 2012, following the two terms (10 years) of President Alpha Konaré who had succeeded Traoré.

10 To cite just a couple of well-known figures, sociologist Aminata Traoré became minister of culture and tourism, while historian Madina Ly Tall headed the Malian embassy in Paris.

11 This is not the place to discuss the ambiguous nature of the democratic transition, whose national conferences were highly publicized events in Africa. Many women participated in them. A select few even participated in decision-making bodies, but it remains unclear what impact they had on the debates and decisions made.

12 Election results from September 2003: 39 women out of 80 deputies.

13 Election results from 1999. The elections held in April 2004 and won by the African National Congress (ANC) are not considered here.

14 Gilchrist Olympio, son of the first president of Togo who was overthrown and assassinated by the current president, is banned from running for office.

15 Among the most active are the Campaign for Good Governance, Federation of African Women Educationists (FAWE), Sierra Leone Association of University Women, and the Federation of Muslim Women's Associations in Sierra Leone (FOMWASIL), among others.

16 He was being challenged by Moustapha Niasse, his previous prime minister.

17 The woman in question is Gertrude Mongella, a former Tanzanian minister and parliamentarian. She was the coordinator of the United Nations World Conference on Women in Nairobi in 1985.

18 In the euphoria of the 1960s, René Dumont was criticized for framing matters in these terms in his searing critique of the new African elites, *L'Afrique noire est mal partie*.

2 Appropriation of Gender Studies in Sub-Saharan Africa

1 This text was initially published in French as "L'appropriation des études sur le genre en Afrique subsaharienne," in Thérèse Locoh (ed.), in collaboration with Koffi Nguessan and Pauline Makinwa-Adebusoye, *Genre et sociétés en Afrique. Implications pour le développement*, Paris: INED, 2007, pp. 47–68.

2 The Decade featured several major international conferences that attracted thousands of attendees: Mexico in 1975, Copenhagen in 1980, and Nairobi in 1985. The 1995 Beijing Conference provided a comprehensive review of the progress made in supporting women and addressing their expectations.

3 Conference on "Urban Security in Africa," UN-Habitat and the United Nations Development Program, Abidjan, July 1997.

4 An order that men established and that they readily question when it no longer suits their own needs.

5 In Islam, maintaining the body's purity is crucial, particularly for women. The presence of various vaginal secretions requires them to perform ritual ablutions before prayers. Additionally, during menstruation, not only is sexual intercourse forbidden, but also women are prohibited from engaging in all religious practices, including praying, fasting and visiting the mosque.

6 The Inter-African Committee on Traditional Practices Affecting the Health of Women and Children (IAC), founded in Dakar in 1984, is a pan-African organization headquartered in Addis Ababa. It maintains national offices across most sub-Saharan African countries where female genital mutilation is prevalent. The organization also issues a periodic publication.

7 Long before the IAC was established, Awa Thiam had already condemned female genital mutilation (FGM) in her book *La parole aux négresses* (1978), which stirred controversy among both men and women. In 1993, the Research, Action, and Information Network for Bodily Integrity of Women (Rainbo), led by Dr. Nahid Toubia from Sudan, was founded with the specific goal of addressing the intersection of health and women's rights, particularly focusing on women's sexual and reproductive rights. That same year marked the launch of a global initiative to combat FGM.

8 This is depicted in Ousmane Sembène's 1960 novel, *God's Bits of Wood* (*Les bouts de bois de Dieu*). The story takes place during a major railway strike, where the strikers' wives embark on a historic 65-kilometer march from Thiès, a crucial railway hub, to Dakar, the capital of the Federation of French West Africa.

9 During the euphoria of the 1960s, René Dumont faced criticism for entitling his book in a manner that sharply criticized the new African elites.

10 Particularly by Moroccan sociologist, Fatima Mernissi, who points out that "the belief held by some Western feminists that Arab women are subservient, obedient slaves who only discovered consciousness-raising and revolutionary ideas when enlightened by the most liberated of all women (feminists from New York, Paris, and London) is less understandable at first sight than the expression of such sentiments by Arab patriarchs" (1984).

11 Among them were Fatima Mernissi from Morocco, Achola Pala from Kenya, Filomena Chioma Steady from Sierra Leone, and Marie-Angélique Savané from Senegal.

12 Oyèrónké Oyéwùmí teaches in the Black Studies department at the University of California, Santa Barbara. Her work received the Distinguished Book Award from the Gender and Sex Section of the American Sociological Association in 1998.

13 The relationships between elders and youth have been extensively studied, particularly in the works of French Marxist anthropology during the 1960s.

14 The debate frequently revolves around the suitability of Western democratic principles – such as voting rights and parliamentary governance – for African societies and for the Global South more broadly. This includes contentious issues like the prohibition of child labor and raises difficult questions such as whether we should legalize the employment of children under 14, who contribute to family incomes in places like Benin, India or Brazil, and help offset economic deficiencies, even if it breaches their rights to education or their basic rights to enjoy childhood.

15 The debate on whether to allow or ban the wearing of the Islamic veil, which has been ongoing in France for the past two decades, is a telling example. Some feminists support the wearing of the veil, arguing that it is a part of cultural identity.

16 Such as, for instance, the Earth Summit (Rio de Janeiro, 1992), the World Conference on Human Rights (Vienna, 1993), the Conference on Population and Development (Cairo, 1994) and the Social Development Summit (Copenhagen, 1995).

17 Most likely to protect them from what Christine Delphy calls "the main enemy" (1998).

18 DAWN (Development Alternatives with Women for a New Era), established in 1984, is a feminist network of women activists, researchers and policymakers from the Global South. It aims to develop alternative frameworks and methods for social and economic justice, peace and development that are free from all

forms of oppression based on sex, class, race or nationality. The coordination of the network is currently based at the University of the South Pacific in Suva, Fiji.

3 Feminist Movements in Africa

1 Originally published as Fatou Sow, "Mouvements féministes en Afrique," in B. Destremau and C. Verschuur (eds.), "Féminismes décoloniaux, genre et développement," *Revue Tiers Monde* 209, special issue, Paris: Armand Colin, Jan.–Mar. 2012, pp. 145–61. [Interview conducted with Blandine Destremau and Christine Verschuur.]

2 President Sarkozy: "The tragedy of Africa is that the African man hasn't yet fully entered into history. The African peasant, who for millennia has lived with the seasons, whose ideal of life is to be in harmony with nature, knows only the eternal return of time marked by the endless repetition of the same actions and the same words. In this worldview, where everything always begins anew, there is no room for human adventure or the idea of progress. In this universe where nature commands everything, man escapes the anguish of history that grips modern man but remains at a standstill within an unchanging order where everything seems to be predestined. Never does man leap toward the future. Never does it occur to him to break out of repetition to shape his own destiny" (Ba Konaré 2008).

3 Women from the ruling Socialist Party and various women's organizations demanded a 25 percent quota of female representatives in parliament.

4 Founded by Annette Mbaye d'Erneville, the first female journalist in Senegal.

5 This is not the place to delve into those critiques. Cf. Bisilliat and Verschuur (2000).

6 The questions of matriarchy and patriarchy have sparked intense debates among many prominent figures, from Lewis H. Morgan to Friedrich Engels, from Cheikh Anta Diop to Françoise Héritier, but they remain beyond the scope of this interview.

4 Female Genital Mutilation and Human Rights in Africa

1 This article first appeared in *Africa Development / Afrique et Développement* 23, 3, 1998.

2 However, as early as 1979, the organization "Choisir," founded by Franco-Tunisian lawyer Gisèle Halimi, had raised awareness about the need to implement laws against sexual mutilation in France.

3 Two recent studies that analyze the practice of genital mutilation and the laws enacted to combat it are essential readings on this matter. First is Jacqueline Smith's *Visions and Discussions on Genital Mutilation of Girls: An International Survey*, published by Defense for Children International, Netherlands, in Amsterdam, May 1995. The second is "Popline Documentation Concerning Female Genital Mutilation," updated in February 1977 by the Population Information Program at the Center for Communication Programs, Johns Hopkins School of Public Health in Baltimore.

4 Sweden is home to populations from Somalia, Eritrea, Ethiopia, Nigeria, Ghana and Gambia. The maximum sentence for such offenses is two years of imprisonment (Smith 1995:170).

5 The Prohibition of Female Circumcision Act, enacted on July 16, 1985, sets a maximum sentence of five years in prison. The Children Act of 1989 further reinforced these measures. Since then, British organizations and members of the African diaspora have launched widespread campaigns to classify female genital mutilation as a human rights violation and an act of violence against girls (Smith 1995:174).

6 Canada was the first country to grant asylum to women on the basis of gender-based violence such as female genital mutilation (March 1994).

7 Solidarity Workshop Against the Practice of Excision, Rainbo and CIAF, Ouagadougou, Burkina Faso, January 28–31, 1997.

8 The Inter-African Committee on Traditional Practices Affecting the Health of Mothers and Children (IAC) has offices in Addis Ababa and Geneva. It oversees the work of national committees in many countries, including the Comité sénégalais contre les pratiques traditionnelles ayant effet sur la santé de la mère et de l'enfant (COSEPRAT) – or the Senegalese Committee Against Traditional Practices Affecting Maternal and Child Health – the Guinean National Committee of the IAC (CPTAFE), the Nigerian Committee Against Traditional Practices Affecting Maternal and Child Health (CONIPRAT) and the National Committee on Traditional Practices of Tanzania (NCTP). The National Committee to Combat the Practice of Excision (CNLPE) in Burkina Faso serves as an administrative body. Additionally, the Inter-African Committee publishes a periodic newsletter.

9 Rainbo (Research, Action, and Information Network for Bodily Integrity of Women), led by Dr. Nahid Toubia from Sudan, is "dedicated to addressing the intersection of health and rights, with

a particular emphasis on women's sexual and reproductive rights." In 1993, the organization launched a global action program aimed at combating female genital mutilation.

10 Various organizations have been established internationally to combat these practices. For example, in the United Kingdom, the Foundation for Women's Health Research and Development and the Women's Health Initiative are notable efforts (as cited by Toubia 1995:6).

11 *Bokk lël*: "shared retreat."

12 Group ceremonies are held at the end of the retreat, drawing family members from various regions. Some of these events, though irregular in their occurrence, also attract onlookers, anthropologists and tourists due to their cultural significance.

13 In Wolof society, every woman must have a *kilifa*, meaning an authority figure within the family, society or religion. *Kilifa* originates from the Arabic word "caliph."

14 See paragraph 96 of the Istanbul Declaration, Habitat II, Istanbul, May–June 1996.

15 The World Food Summit, FAO, Rome, 1996.

16 Fact Sheet No. 22, Discrimination against Women: The Convention and the Committee, Human Rights Series, Global Campaign for Human Rights, Human Rights Center, United Nations, Geneva and New York (1995).

17 The workshop was organized by ENDA-ACAS (Senegal), the Djoliba Center (Mali), Rädda Barnen (Sweden) and SNV (a Dutch development organization). Participants came from Senegal, Mali, Guinea-Bissau, Guinea-Conakry, Gambia, Mauritania, Burkina Faso and Côte d'Ivoire.

18 In July 1997, the organizations Sisterhood Is Global and Women Living Under Muslim Laws initiated an international campaign to denounce these measures.

5 Who Owns Women's Bodies?

1 This chapter is taken from a talk delivered by Fatou Sow, at the Symposium on "Sexual and Reproductive Health in Southern Countries," held during the 26th Pharo Developments 2021 (Actualités du Pharo), Groupe d'intervention en santé publique et épidémiologie (GISPE), La Timone Hospital, Marseille, October 6–8, 2021.

2 General Commission for Terminology and Neology: Recommendation on French equivalents for the word "gender," dated July 22, 2005, *Official Journal* of the French Republic of July 22, 2005 MCC. See www.education.gouv.fr/bo/2005/34/CTNX0508542X.htm.

3 The book was published under the title *Notre corps, notre santé. Santé et sexualité des femmes en Afrique subsaharienne*, ed. Fatou Sow and Codou Bop, Paris: L'Harmattan, 2004.

4 *Dammel, Buur, Brak, Teeñ, Almaami, Seriñ* are titles in Senegal given to sovereigns or religious leaders (with the advent of Islamization). *Lingueer* are aristocratic women, specifically the mothers, sisters and daughters of ruling families.

5 Mabingué Ngom, originally from Senegal, was appointed in 2022 as the director of the United Nations Population Fund (UNFPA) at the African Union (AU) and the United Nations Economic Commission for Africa (ECA).

6 Many polygamous husbands refuse to wear condoms. In Dakar, a young woman who labeled polygamy as a form of multi-partner sexual relationship was almost lynched in her own neighborhood.

6 Religion and Politics in Sub-Saharan African Secular States

1 "Religion and Politics in Sub-Saharan African Secular States," talk given by Fatou Sow, at the International Conference on "The Religious-Right, Secularism and Civil Rights" held in London, October 11–12, 2014.

2 The British Empire later attempted to codify these so-called customary laws in several of its colonies, as it had previously done in India.

3 Almaami (also spelled Almamy or Almami) is the title given to Muslim sovereigns of the Fulani states in West Africa (Senegal River Valley, Guinea, Niger, etc.).

4 Religious brotherhoods have largely taken over the political power that existed in the pre-colonial period.

5 This population, also known as Black Moors, is Arabic-speaking.

6 "Biram Ould Abeid and six of his activist associates were charged on May 3 [2012] for, among other things, 'violating Islamic values.' On April 27, they had burned foundational texts of the Maliki school in Nouakchott, including works by Ibn Achir, Al-Akhdari and Khalil, which they accused of validating slavery. Such an act is punishable by up to 30 years in prison in Mauritania" (*Jeune Afrique*, September 4, 2012). Biram Ould Abeid is the founder of the Initiative for the Resurgence of the Abolitionist Movement (IRA).

7 Let's not forget that their monarch, who leads the kingdom, also serves as the head of the Anglican Church.

8 The 2000 elections marked the defeat of the Socialist Party, which

had been in power since independence in 1960, totaling 40 years of uninterrupted rule.

7 The Representation of Women and Claims to Citizens' Rights in Africa: Beyond a Political Debate

1 Institute's 2019 Biennial Lecture, delivered by Fatou Sow on June 11 at the 8th European African Studies Conference (ECAS 8), "Africa: Connections and Disruptions," International Africa Institute, Edinburgh, June 12–14, 2019.

8 What Secularism Means for African Women's Rights and Citizenship

1 Lecture at the Colloquium on "What Secularism Means to Africa: What It Has Been, What It Hadn't Been, and What It Could Mean for Human Rights," Nairobi, August 24–25, 2016. The proceedings were published under the same title by Catholics for Choice in collaboration with the Global Interfaith and Secular Alliance.

References

Adesina, Jimi. "Re-appropriating Matrifocality: Endogeneity and African Gender Scholarship," *African Sociological Review*, 14 (1), 2010, pp. 2–19.

African Feminist Forum. *The Charter of Feminist Principles for African Feminists / La charte des principes féministes pour les féministes africaines*, 2006, www.fr.africanfeministforum .com/the-charter-of-feminist-principles-for-African-Feminists.

Akpaki, Roger Soumon. "Dynamique économique des femmes et mutations socio-politiques au Sud du Bénin et au Sud-Ouest du Nigeria de 1946 à 1990." Doctoral thesis, vol. 1, Université Paris-VII – Denis Diderot, 2001.

Amadiume, Ifi. *Male Daughters, Female Husbands: Gender and Sex in an African Society*. London: Zed Books, 1987.

Amadiume, Ifi. "Contemporary Women's Organisations: Contradictions and Irrelevance in the Struggle for Grassroots Participatory Democracy in Nigeria." Paper presented at the Colloquium on "Social Movements, Social Transformations and the Struggle for Democracy in Africa," CODESRIA, Tunis, May 21–23, 1990.

Amadiume, Ifi. *Re-inventing Africa: Matriarchy, Religion and Culture*. London: Zed Books, 1997.

Antrobus, Peggy. *The Global Women's Movement: Origins, Issues and Strategies*. A Brave New Series: Global Issues in a Changing World. London: Zed Books, 2004.

Assié-Lumumba, Ndri. "Le genre dans la recherche en Afrique," *Echo*, n.s., 5, 2000.

Assié-Lumumba, Ndri. *Les Africaines dans la politique: femmes Baoulé de Côte d'Ivoire*. Points de Vue. Paris: L'Harmattan, 1996.

Attoe, Effah. *Women in National Development of Nigeria since Precolonial Times*, 1996. www.onlinenigeria.com/links.

Ba, Mame Penda. "La diversité du fondamentalisme sénégalais: éléments pour une sociologie de la connaissance." *Cahiers d'études africaines*, 206–7, 2012, pp. 575–602.

Ba Konaré, Adam. *Dictionnaire des femmes célèbres du Mali*. Bamako: Éditions Jamana, 1993.

Ba Konaré, Adam (ed.). *Petit précis de remise à niveau sur l'histoire africaine à l'usage du président Sarkozy*. Paris: La Découverte, 2008.

Badawi Abbas, Zeinab. "Needed Reforms in Family Muslim Laws and Customary Laws in Sudan." In Tire Akolda Man and Balghis Badri (eds.), *Law Reform in Sudan*. Omdurman: Ahfad University for Women, 2008, pp. 207–37.

Bakare-Yusuf, Bibi. "Yorubas Don't Do Gender: A Critical Review of Oyèrónké Oyéwùmí's *The Invention of Women: Making an African Sense of Western Gender Discourses*." Paper presented at the CODESRIA Colloquium on "African Gender Research in the New Millennium: Perspectives, Directions and Challenges," Cairo, May 2002.

Bakare-Yusuf, Bibi. "Yorubas Don't Do Gender: A Critical Review of Oyeronke Oyewumi's The Invention of Women: Making an African Sense of Western Gender Discourses," *Feminist Africa*, 2, 2003, pp. 1–17.

Barilier, Etienne. *Le droit maternel: recherche sur la gynécocratie de l'Antiquité dans sa nature religieuse et juridique*. Lausanne and Paris: Éditions l'Âge de l'homme, 1996. (Translation from German of Johan Bachofen, *Das Mutterrecht*, 1861.)

Baubérot, Jean. *Histoire de la laïcité en France*. Paris: Presses Universitaires de France, 1990.

Baubérot, Jean. "Laïcité(s), sécularisation(s). Quelques hypothèses." Working paper for the Colloquium on "Sécularisations et laïcités en Asie," Groupe Sociétés, Religions, Laïcités de l'EHSS, Paris, June 26–27, 2014. www .gsrl.cnrs.fr/sites/gsrl/img/pdf./colloque_secularisations_et _laicites_en_asie_GSRL-pdf.

Baubérot, Jean, Dominique Borne, Jean-Paul Delahaye and Henri Pena-Ruiz (eds.). "État, laïcité, religions," *La Documentation française*, Coll. Regards sur l'actualité, 298, 2004.

Bencheikh, Ghaleb. *La laïcité au regard du Coran*. Paris: Presses de la Renaissance, 2005.

Bennoune, Karima. *Your Fatwa Does Not Apply Here: Untold Stories from the Fight against Muslim Fundamentalism*. New York: W. W. Norton, 2013.

Binka, Charlotte. "Confronting the Challenges: Women in Ghanaian Politics," 1996, www.lolapress.org/artenglish /bine10_5.htm.

Bisilliat, Jeanne, and Christine Verschuur (eds.). "Le genre: un outil nécessaire. Introduction à une problématique," *Cahiers Genre et développement*. Paris: L'Harmattan, No. 1, February 2000.

Boahen, A. Adu. *African Perspectives on Colonialism*. Baltimore: Johns Hopkins University Press, 1987.

Bop, Codou. "Les violences à l'égard des femmes en République de Guinée-Conakry." In Fatou Sow, Codou Bop and Fatou Sarr, *Violences, droits et politique: les cas des femmes de Sierra Leone, Côte d'Ivoire et Guinée-Conakry*. London: Interights, 2001.

Brossier, Marie. "Les débats sur la réforme du code de la famille au Sénégal: la redéfinition de la laïcité comme enjeu du processus de démocratisation." Mémoire de DEA, Université Paris 1 Panthéon–Sorbonne, 2004.

Busia, Abena (ed.). "Introduction." In *Gender Violence and Women's Human Rights in Africa*. New Brunswick, NJ: Center for Women's Global Leadership, 1994, pp. i–iv.

Carby, Hazel. "White Woman Listen! Black Feminism and the Boundaries of Sisterhood." In *The Empire Strikes Back: Race and Racism in Seventies Britain*. Center for Contemporary Cultural Studies. London: Hutchinson, 1982, pp. 212–35.

Castells, Manuel. *Le pouvoir de l'identité*. Paris: Fayard, 1999. (Translated from English by P. Chemla, *The Power of Identity*. Malden, MA: Blackwell Publishers, 1997.)

Coulon, Christian. "Introduction: les nouvelles voies de l'umma africaine," *Politique africaine*, 2002, pp. 19–29.

Crenshaw, Kimberlé. "Cartographies des marges: intersection-nalité, politique de l'identité et violences contre les femmes de couleur," *Cahiers du Genre*, 39, 2005. (Translation of "Mapping the Margins: Intersectionality, Identity Politics, and Violence against Women of Color." In Martha Albertson Fineman and Rixanne Mykitiuk [eds.], *The Public Nature of Private Violence*. New York: Routledge, 1994.)

Degni, Segui. "État de droit, droit de l'homme. Bilan de dix années." In *Rapport sur l'état des pratiques de la démocratie, des droits et des libertés dans l'espace francophone, Bamako, dix ans 2000–2010*, Délégation à la paix, à la démocratie et aux droits de l'homme, Paris, Organisation internationale de la Francophonie, 2010, www.democratie.francophonie .org/rapport_observatoire_2010/projet/rapport-francophonie -2010.pdf.

Delphy, Christine. *L'ennemi principal*, Vol. I: *Économie politique du patriarcat*. Paris: Éditions Syllepse, 1998, 2009, 2013.

Delphy, Christine. *L'ennemi principal*, Vol. II: *Penser le genre*. Paris: Éditions Syllepse, 2001, 2009, 2013.

Desroches-Noblecourt, Christiane. *La femme au temps des Pharaons*. Paris: Stock, 1986.

Destremau, Blandine, and Christine Verschuur. "Mouvements féministes en Afrique." Interview with Fatou Sow, in "Féminismes décoloniaux et développement," *Revue Tiers Monde*, Armand Colin, 209, 2012/1, pp. 145–60.

Diaw, Aminata, and Aminata Touré. *Femme, éthique et politique*. Dakar: Fondation Friedrich Ebert, 1998.

Diop, Cheikh Anta. *L'unité culturelle de l'Afrique noire: domaines du patriarcat et du matriarcat dans l'Antiquité classique*. Paris: Présence africaine, 1981 [1959].

Diop, Abdoulaye Bara. *La famille wolof*. Paris: Karthala, 1985.

Dumont, René. *L'Afrique noire est mal partie*. Paris: Le Seuil, Points, 1962.

Erlich, Michel. "Notion de mutilation sexuelle," *Droit et Cultures*, 1990.

Falquet, Jules. "Femmes, féminisme et 'développement': une analyse critique des politiques des institutions internationales." In Jeanne Bisilliat (ed.), *Regards de femmes sur la globalisation. Approches critiques*. Paris: Karthala, 2003, pp. 75–112.

Fricke, Adrienne L., with Amira Khair. *Law without Justice: An Assessment of Sudanese Laws Affecting Survivors of Rape*. Washington, DC: Refugees International, 2007.

Friedan, Betty. *The Feminine Mystique*. New York: W. W. Norton and Company, 1963.

Gomez-Perez, Muriel (ed.). *L'islam politique au sud du Sahara. Identités, discours et enjeux.* Paris: Karthala, 2005.

Guillaume, Sophie. "Les femmes guinéennes sous Sékou Touré (1958–1984)." Mémoire de DEA, Université Paris Diderot, Paris, Sept. 2000.

Hélie-Lucas, Marième (ed.). "The Struggle for Secularism in Europe and North America: Women from Migrant Descent Facing the Rise of Fundamentalism," *WLUML Dossier* 30–1, 2011.

Hill-Collins, Patricia. *Black Feminist Thought: Knowledge, Consciousness, and the Politics of Empowerment.* New York and London: Routledge, 1990.

hooks, bell. *Ain't I a Woman: Black Women and Feminism.* Boston: South End Press, 1981.

Horn, Jessica. "Not 'Culture' but Gender: Reconceptualising Female Genital Mutilation/Cutting." In Wendy Chavkin and Ellen Chesler (eds.), *Where Human Rights Begin: Health, Sexuality and Women Ten Years after Vienna, Cairo, and Beijing.* New Jersey: Rutgers University Press, 2005.

Hosken, Fran. 1993. *The Hosken Report,* 4th edn. Lexington, MA: WIN News.

Imam, Ayesha, Amina Mama and Fatou Sow (eds.). *Engendering African Social Sciences.* Dakar: CODESRIA, 1997.

Jacq, Christian. *Les Égyptiennes.* Paris: Perrin, 1996.

Kandji, Saliou, and Fatou-Kiné Camara. *L'union matrimoniale dans la tradition des peuples noirs.* Paris: L'Harmattan, 2000.

Kane, Cheikh Hamidou. *L'aventure ambiguë.* Paris: Julliard, 1961.

Kéita, Aoua. *Femme d'Afrique. La vie d'Aoua Kéita, racontée par elle-même.* Paris: Présence africaine, 1975.

Kouyaté Carvalho, Henriette. "Les mutilations sexuelles," *Vie et Santé, Revue de Réseau de Recherche en Santé de la Reproduction en Afrique francophone,* 4, July 1990.

"Lettre ouverte au Président de la République du Mali. Les ONG signataires demandent la non-promulgation du Code de la famille." www.fidh.org/Le-code-de-la-famille-ne-doit-pas, January 21, 2012.

Lewis, Desiree. "African Gender Women's Studies: 1980–2002," *Feminist Africa,* 1, 2002, pp. 15–38.

Löwy, Ilana, and Hélène Rouch. "La distinction entre sexe et genre. Une histoire entre biologie et culture," *Cahiers du Genre,* 34, 2003.

Mama, Amina. "Études par les femmes et études sur les femmes en Afrique durant les années 1990" / "Women's Studies and Studies of Women in Africa during the 1990s." Working Paper 5/96. Dakar: CODESRIA, 1996.

Mama, Amina. "Editorial." *Feminist Africa*, 1, 5, 2002, pp. 1–8.

Mama, Amina. "Gender Studies for Africa's Transformation: Intellectuals, Nationalism and the Pan-African Ideal," Grand Finale Conference, 30th anniversary of CODESRIA, Dakar, December 10-12, 2003, unpublished.

Mama, Amina. "Demythologising Gender in Development: Feminist Studies in African Contexts." *IDS Bulletin*, 35, 4, 2004, pp. 121–4.

Mama, Amina. "Feminism: Africa, and the Diaspora." In Maryanne Cline Horowitz (ed.), *New Dictionary of the History of Ideas*, Vol. II. Detroit: Charles Scribner's Sons, 2005.

Marchal, Roland. "Le Soudan d'un conflit à l'autre." *Les Études du CERI, Fondation nationale des sciences politiques*, 107–8, Sept. 2004, www.sciencespo.fr/ceri/sites/ sciencespo.fr.ceri /files/etude107.pdf.

Mathieu, Nicole-Claude (ed.). *L'arraisonnement des femmes, Essais en anthropologie des sexes*, Cahiers de l'Homme 24. Paris: Éditions de l'EHESS, 1985.

Mazrui, Ali. "Shariacracy and the Federal Modes in the Era of Globalisation: Nigeria in Comparative Perspective," paper presented at the International Conference on the Restoration of Shariah in Nigeria: Challenges and Benefits, London, 2001.

Mbow, Penda (ed.). *Hommes et femmes entre sphères publique et privée*. Gender 5. Dakar: CODESRIA, 2005.

Mbow, Penda. "The Secular State and Citizenship in Muslim Countries: Bringing Africa into the Debate." In Cassandra Balchin (ed.), *Exploring Secularisms, Religion, and Patriarchy*. *WLUML Dossier* 28, 2008.

McFadden, Patricia. "The Challenge and Prospects for the African Women's Movement in the 21st Century," *Women in Action*, The Human Rights Information Network (HURIN), 1, 1997, www.hartford-hwp.com/archives/30/152.html.

Mernissi, Fatima. "The Merchant's Daughter and the Son of the Sultan." In Robin Morgan (ed.), *Sisterhood Is Global: The International Women's Movement Anthology*. New York: Anchor Press and Doubleday, 1984, pp. 447–54.

Michel, Andrée, Agnès-Fatoumata Diarra and Hélène Dos

Santos-Agbessy (eds.). *Femmes et multinationales*. Paris: ACCT and Karthala, 1981.

Mies, Maria. *Patriarchy and Accumulation on a World Scale. Women in the International Division of Labour*. New York: Zed Books, 1998 [1986].

Millet, Kate. *La politique du mâle*. Paris: Stock, 1971.

Monga, Célestin. *L'anthropologie de la colère, société civile et démocratie en Afrique noire*. Paris: L'Harmattan, 1995.

Mottin-Sylla, Marie-Hélène. *L'argent et l'intérêt. Tontines et autres pratiques féminines de mobilisation à Dakar*. Dakar: ENDA-GRAF, 1987.

Moya, Ismaël. "De l'argent aux valeurs. Femmes, économie, parenté et islam à Thiaroye-sur-Mer, Dakar, Sénégal." Doctoral thesis, Paris, EHESS, 2011.

N'Diaye, Marième. "Sénégal – Marième N'Diaye sur la dépénalisation de l'avortement: 'Le débat est ouvert,'" *Le Point Afrique*, April 11, 2019. Accessible via HAL: hal-02531548.

Ngom, Mabingué. "La capture du dividende démographique. Développement: les voies africaines," *Politique Internationale*, 165, 2019.

Ngom, Mabingué. *La capture du dividende démographique au service de l'émergence: cas de la commune de Gueule Tapée-Fass-Colobane (Dakar)*. Paris: L'Harmattan, 2021.

Niang, Babacar. 2002. *Pour un Code du Statut Personnel au Sénégal*. Dakar: CIRCOFS.

Nzegwu, Nkiru. "Globalization and the *Jenda* Journal." *Jenda, A Journal of Culture and African Women Studies*, "Feminism and Africa," 1 (1), 2001, www.jendajournal.com.

Osha, Sanya. "African Feminisms," *Quest: An African Journal of Philosophy*, 20 (1–2), 2006.

Oyéwùmí, Oyèrónké. *The Invention of Women: Making an African Sense of Western Gender Discourses*. Minneapolis: University of Minnesota Press, 1997.

Oyéwùmí, Oyèrónké. "Family Bonds / Conceptual Binds: African Notes on Feminist Epistemologies," *Signs*, "Feminism at a Millennium," 25 (4), 2000, pp. 1093–8.

Oyéwùmí, Oyèrónké. "Conceptualizing Gender: The Eurocentric Foundations of Feminist Concepts and the Challenge of African Epistemologies." *Jenda, A Journal of Culture and African Women Studies*, "Feminism and Africa," 2 (1), 2002.

Oyéwùmí, Oyèrónké. "Abiyamo: Theorizing African

Motherhood," *Jenda, A Journal of Culture and African Women Studies*, 4, 2003.

Pala, Achola, and Madina Ly. *La Femme africaine dans la société précoloniale.* Paris: UNESCO, 1979.

Report of the Fourth World Conference on Women, Beijing, September 4–15, 1995.

Rogers, Barbara. *The Domestication of Women: Discrimination in Developing Societies.* London: Kogan Ltd; New York: St. Martin's Press, 1980.

Salo, Elaine, and Pumla Dineo Gqola. "Editorial: Subaltern Sexualities," *Feminist Africa*, 6, 2006, pp. 1–11.

Sanankoua, Bintou. "Femmes, Islam et droit de la famille au Mali." Paper presented at the international colloquium on "L'Islam dans les sociétés de l'Afrique subsaharienne: défis et réponses," Dakar, February 4–8, 2008.

Sembène, Ousmane. *Les bouts de bois de Dieu.* Paris: Pocket, 2013 [1960].

Semin, Jeanne. "Mise en scène d'une oikonomia africaine: Tontines et cérémonies chez les Wolof, Khassonké et dans la diaspora." Doctoral thesis, Paris, EHESS, 2011.

Smith, Jacqueline. *Visions and Discussions on Genital Mutilation of Girls: An International Survey.* Amsterdam: Defence for Children International, Netherlands, May 1995.

SAC (Société africaine de culture). *La civilisation de la femme dans la tradition africaine.* Paris: Présence africaine, 1975.

SAC (Société africaine de culture). *La femme noire dans la vie moderne, images et réalités.* Paris: Présence africaine, 141, 1987.

Sow, Fatou. "Femmes, socialité et valeurs africaines," *Notes africaines*, 168, 1975, pp. 105–12.

Sow, Fatou. "La cinquième conférence régionale africaine des femmes de Dakar," *Recherches féministes*, 8 (1), 1995, pp. 175–83.

Sow, Fatou. "Les femmes, le sexe de l'État et les enjeux du politique en Afrique: l'exemple de la régionalisation au Sénégal," *Clio, Histoire, femmes et sociétés*, special issue "Femmes d'Afrique," 6, 1997, pp. 127–44.

Sow, Fatou. "Penser les femmes et l'islam en Afrique: une approche féministe." In Odile Georg and Chantal Chanson-Jabeur (eds.), *Mama Africa, Mélanges offerts à Catherine Coquery-Vidrovitch.* Paris: L'Harmattan, 2005, pp. 335–57.

Sow, Fatou. "L'appropriation des études sur le genre en Afrique subsaharienne." In Thérèse Locoh et al. (eds.), *Genre et sociétés en Afrique. Implications pour le développement.* Paris: INED, 2007, pp. 47–68.

Sow, Fatou (ed.). *Genre et fondamentalismes.* Dakar: CODESRIA, 2018.

Sow, Fatou, and Codou Bop (eds.). *Notre corps, notre santé. Santé et sexualité des femmes en Afrique subsaharienne.* Paris: L'Harmattan, 2004.

Sow, Fatou, and Mamadou Guèye. *Les Sénégalaises en chiffres. Étude sur les données socio-économique relatives aux femmes.* Dakar: PNUD, 2000.

Sow, Fatou, and Magali Pazello. "The Making of a Secular Contract." In Gita Sen and Marina Durano (eds.), for DAWN, *The Remaking of Social Contracts: Feminists in a Fierce New World.* London: Zed Books, 2014, pp. 181–95.

Steady, Filomena Chioma (ed.). *The Black Woman Cross-Culturally.* Cambridge, MA: Schenkman, 1981.

Steady, Filomena Chioma. "An Investigative Framework for Gender Research in Africa in the New Millennium." Paper presented at the CODESRIA colloquium on "African Gender Research in the New Millennium: Perspectives, Directions and Challenges," Cairo, May 2002.

Steady, Filomina Chioma. "An Investigative Framework for Gender Research in Africa in the New Millennium." In Oyèrónké Oyéwùmí (ed.), *African Gender Studies: Conceptual and Theoretical Issues.* London: Palgrave, 2005.

Suberu, Rotimi. "Nigeria's Shari'a Debates." In Muriel Gomez-Perez (ed.), *L'islam politique au sud du Sahara. Identités, discours et enjeux.* Paris: Karthala, 2005, pp. 209–26.

Sudarkasa, Niara. *The Strength of Our Mothers: African and African American Women and Families. Essays and Speeches.* New York: Africa World Press, 1997.

Sutherland-Addy, Essy, and Aminata Diaw (eds.). *Des femmes écrivent l'Afrique: l'Afrique de l'Ouest et le Sahel,* Vol. II. Paris: Karthala, 2007.

Tamale, Sylvia. "Gender Trauma in Africa: Enhancing Women's Links to Resources." In *Gender, Economies and Entitlements in Africa.* CODESRIA Gender Series. Dakar: CODESRIA, 2004, pp. 18–31.

Tamale, Sylvia. "Eroticism, Sensuality and 'Women's Secrets' among the Baganda." *Feminist Africa*, "Sexuality Matters," 5, 2006, pp. 89–105.

Taylor, Viviene (ed.). *La marchandisation de la gouvernance*. Paris: L'Harmattan, 2002. (French version of *The Marketisation of Governance*, Cape Town: DAWN, 2000, translated from English by Fatou Sow.)

Tsikata, Dzodzi. "Gender Equality and the State in Ghana: Some Issues of Policy and Practice." In Ayesha Imam, Amina Mama and Fatou Sow (eds.), *Engendering African Social Sciences*. Dakar: CODESRIA, 1997.

Ufomata, Titi. "Linguistic Images, Socialization and Gender in Education." In Fatou Sow (ed.). "Gender Revisited." *Africa Development/Afrique et Développement*. Dakar: CODESRIA, Vol. 23, No. 3–4, 1998, pp. 61–75.

Urdang, Stephanie. *And They Still Dance: Women, War, and the Struggle for Change in Mozambique*. New York: Monthly Review Press, 1989.

Walker, Anne. "The Women's Movement and its Role in Development." In Jane Parpart, Patricia Conelly and Eudine V. Barriteau (eds.), *Theoretical Perspectives on Gender and Development*. Ottawa: IDRC, 2000, pp. 191–202.

"Women in National Parliaments," www.ipu.org/wmn-e/world.

Administrative Documents

Central African Republic, Law No. 13.001, portant "Charte constitutionnelle de transition," July 18, 2013, www.primature -rca.org/constitution.asp.

Constitution de la Côte d'Ivoire, July 23, 2000, www.democratie .francophonie.org/IMG/pdf/Cote_d_Ivoire, pdf.

Constitution du Tchad (revised), March 31, 1996, www .presidencetchad.org/Constitution_Tchad, pdf.

Constitution of Kenya, revised (2010), www.kenyaembassy.com /pdfs/The_Constitution_Kenya, pdf.

Constitution of Republic of Ghana, 1992, www.ghanaweb.com /GhanaHomePage/republic/constitution.php.

Constitution of Sierra Leone, 1991, www.statehouse-sl.org /constitution.

Constitution of South Africa, 1996, www.gov.za/documents /constitution-republic-africa-1996-preamble.

Constitution of Uganda, 2005, www.statehouse.go.ug/sites /default/files/attachments/ abridged_constitution_2006.pdf.

Constitution of United Republic of Tanzania, 1997, www .judiciary.go.tz.

Fact Sheet No. 22, "Discrimination Against Women: The Convention and the Committee," Human Rights Series. Geneva and New York: Global Campaign for Human Rights, Human Rights Center, United Nations, 1995.

"Islams d'Afrique: entre le local et le global," L'Afrique politique, Paris: Karthala, 2002.

"Rapport initial, deuxième et troisième Rapports combinés relatifs à la mise en œuvre de la Convention sur l'élimination de toutes les formes de discrimination à l'égard des femmes en République de Guinée. Ministère des Affaires sociales, de la promotion féminine et de l'enfance," Conakry, Nov. 1998.